STYLES OF THINKING

Also by Robert M. Bramson
COPING WITH DIFFICULT PEOPLE

Allen F. Harrison and Robert M. Bramson, Ph.D.

STYLES OF THINKING

Strategies for Asking Questions,
Making Decisions, and Solving Problems

1982

Anchor Press/Doubleday

Garden City, New York

The Anchor Press edition is the first publication of STYLES OF THINKING

Anchor Press Edition 1982

Library of Congress Cataloging in Publication Data

Harrison, Allen F.
  Styles of thinking.

  1. Thought and thinking. 2. Questioning.
3. Decision-making. 4. Problem solving. I. Bramson,
Robert. II. Title.
B105.T54H37   153.4'2
ISBN 0-385-15763-0   AACR2
Library of Congress Catalog Card Number 80-1095

FOREWORD

The work that we do and that which has gone into this book is practical and applied. We do not conduct our research in a laboratory, using closely controlled experiments, nor are we theoreticians, methodically building a framework of knowledge and hypotheses through rigorous analysis of the work of previous thinkers and researchers.

Yet, our method and approach is not without a long tradition in science. Field biologists, for example, look at insects or birds in their natural settings. They observe, analyze behavior, develop categories, and try to arrive at some useful generalizations about their subjects, as they lead their everyday lives.

Our field studies happen to focus on people as they go about their business with others. In doing this we look for those perspectives that will help us to understand their behavior and to draw some useful generalizations about it; and for tools that will help in measuring and differentiating that behavior.

Much of our findings is presented in anecdotal form, stemming directly from observation on our part or from the accounts of others. In that sense, our work is purely empirical, including the methods we use to test our ideas—such as the I_nQ, the questionnaire that we have developed to measure preferences in Styles of Thinking (which will be found later in the book).

A great deal of the material contained in this book draws richly from the work of others. We want to acknowledge those debts.

The basic framework for our general approach to Styles of Thinking and for the I_nQ derives largely from the work of C.

West Churchman, Professor of Business Administration at the University of California, Berkeley. Professor Churchman's earlier work was in the application of quantified methods to organizational behavior and management. In recent years, he has turned his attention to broader issues of behavior and inquiry. In his book, *The Design of Inquiring Systems,* he identified five Inquiry Modes and their philosophical and historical roots.

Ian Mitroff of the University of Pittsburgh, with various associates, expanded upon Dr. Churchman's work and put it into operational terms. To Dr. Mitroff we owe the rubrics that we have used for our five Styles of Thinking.

In a more general way, we were influenced by the work on thinking and individual differences in cognitive styles of George A. Kelly, George S. Klein, Jerome Bruner and associates; and by the writings of Erich Fromm, Carl Jung, Jean Piaget, Justus Buchler, and Robert Ornstein. Many of the things we say about motivation were prompted by Gordon Alport, Abraham Maslow, David McClelland and William Schutz.

Among colleagues known to one or both of us, or with whom we have worked, we owe a debt for ideas and insights to Pauline K. Arneberg, Neely D. Gardner, David E. Hartl, James March, Frank O. Mason, Raymond E. Miles, Alberto Guerrero Ramos, John P. van Gigch, Jack London, Paul Takagi, and James F. T. Bugenthal. We are particularly indebted to those with whom we have worked for years in the measurement of stylistic preferences: Stuart Atkins, Allan Katcher, and Elias Porter, Jr.

Our business partners, G. Nicholas Parlette and Susan J. Bramson, have been instrumental in the development of the I_nQ, in contributing ideas and time to our research, and in tolerating and encouraging our sometimes erratic Synthesist behavior. In particular, the content of Chapter IX on methods for influencing others bears the stamp of Susan's caring and practical insights from her own managerial and consulting experience.

Especially intimate notes of thanks go to Robert Bramson's son, Rob, for his statistical work and general help in focusing our inquiry; and to Allen Harrison's wife, Audrey Ross, a superb editor and critic, who taught her husband so much about how to write clearly.

A specific acknowledgment should be made to the Western Consortium for Continuing Education for the Health Professions, Inc., which provided funding for some of the development and the initial testing of the I_nQ; and to the National Training and Development Service, especially Charles "Chip" Morrison, for providing an early opportunity for exposure to our ideas.

Most importantly, though, we acknowledge the single contribution without which we could not have done our work or written this book: that of our clients, many of whom are also our friends, who continue not only to suffer but to welcome and even pay for our curiosity about them.

CONTENTS

All thinking is based, in part, on prior convictions.

George A. Kelly

STYLES OF THINKING

Chapter I

THINKING ABOUT THINKING—
AN INTRODUCTION

People think about things in different ways

Most people, most of the time, think about things in only one way. Some people occasionally use two ways of thinking. Very few people ever approach a situation in more than two ways. Almost no one, whether a one-way or a two-way thinker, understands his or her limitations. All of us think about things the way we do because it is the "right" way.

When we approach problems or decisions, we employ a set of specific strategies, whether we know it or not. Each of us has a preference for a limited set of thinking strategies. Each set of strategies has its strengths and liabilities. Each is useful in a given situation, but each can be catastrophic if overused or used inappropriately. Yet almost all of us learn only one or two sets of strategies, and we go through life using them no matter the situation.

All around us we see people achieving success using strategies very different from our own, but despite the evidence we persist in the ways that we believe work for us. We impose our own limitations, and we find it hard to understand those who persist in *their* own peculiar methods.

When we succeed in our efforts, we are pleased because our values are confirmed. When we fail, we rationalize and, most often, blame others for our failure or ascribe it to plain bad luck. We seldom take the trouble to learn new ways of thinking. If we were to do so, we would expand our adaptability to problem situations and to the events of daily life.

Why This Book Was Written

This is a book about how to make fewer stupid decisions. It is also about expanding your repertoire of strategies for asking questions, making decisions, solving problems, and getting along better with all those odd people who do things differently from you.

As practitioners in the behavioral sciences, consultants and teachers, we have worked with individuals and groups in all walks of life but particularly in formal organizations. Most of our work can be described in two general ways: helping people ask better questions, in order to make better decisions and solve problems more efficiently; and helping people work together and communicate more effectively.

It doesn't seem to matter how much people like each other, or how well they get along together, or how agreeable their personalities are. When it comes to a matter of solving a problem or making a decision, any two people, chosen at random, are not only likely to approach the situation differently, but they seem to be looking at two very different situations. When a problem-solving group is made up of six, twelve, or fifty people, the situation becomes quite bewildering. It's no wonder so many people say they hate meetings!

Confronted again and again by such observations in our work, we spent a great deal of time pointing out to people that their procedures in problem solving were indeed different. But all they had to do, we used to say, was allow for their differences in procedure and try to negotiate an understanding on their goals, on the end result of whatever it was they were trying to work out. If people would only agree on goals, then the rest of it would follow, because the differences and the conflicts were merely about matters of approach. They were differences in means, not ends.

We were wrong. But we were right, too.

We were right in understanding that the problems people experience with each other derive from differences in approach. What we failed to understand, for a long time, was how fundamental such differences are.

We were wrong in our insistence that, "If we can just agree on the goals, everything else will follow." That statement, we realize now, is itself a statement about an approach and a set of values. It is a statement about a particular thinking strategy, which happens to be the one we now call the strategy of the Idealist.

Thus we began an investigation that led us to the notion that the way people think about things might be the basic key to individual differences, interlinked with, but more fundamental than, differences in personality. We read widely what others have written about thinking and became more convinced that thinking strategically might not be merely something people do in order to solve problems and make decisions, but something they do because that is the way people are constructed.

Our first need was to acquire a framework with which to describe the various Styles of Thinking and a means of measuring and testing individual preferences for them. We then tested the practicality and usefulness of both the ideas and the measuring device with a large number of clients and associates. The testing showed them to be of such value that writing this book seemed almost a necessity.

What You Can Learn from This Book

Once you have read this book, taken the exercises that are included in it, and practiced some of the steps that we recommend, you should realize a number of useful benefits.

First, you will understand your own Style of Thinking, the styles of other people who are important to you, and the differences between them. Once you know your own preferences in approach and those of others—and can recognize the differences—you will have a springboard toward becoming a more adaptable and versatile problem solver, not only in terms of day-to-day situations but in terms of your working relationships with others.

Second, you will be able to identify your own blind spots. You will learn to recognize the errors into which your preferred Style of Thinking is likely to lead you, and the kinds of situations in which they occur. Once you have this kind of knowledge, it is a relatively easy task to learn to compensate for your blind spots and to avoid errors—not all the time, of course, but more often than you do now.

Third, you will learn how to use your existing strengths more productively. We are not interested in changing you, or even in changing your basic approach to life and the world. Your existing strengths are vital and essential to you. What you will get from this book are some useful ideas about making your strengths work for you more manageably and effectively.

Fourth, you will learn a number of practical and accessible methods for augmenting and expanding your Style of Thinking. That is, you will be able to broaden your repertoire. You can acquire new strategies for approaching work and life situations more productively, leading to enhanced individual success and improved relations with others.

Fifth, you will learn some specific methods for influencing and communicating with others in the most effective way.

Chapter II

STYLES OF THINKING—
THE i_nQ

The Basic Question

How do you think about things?

Most people find this an extremely difficult question to answer. Confronted with such a question, the typical response, we have found, is a surprised stare, a blank look, and perhaps words like these:

"What do you mean, how do I think about things? I just *think*, that's all, like anybody else does. Like any human being does."

To answer the question— How do you think about things?—is difficult if not impossible, because, for most of us, it is a completely new question.

Yet it is exactly that question that we have been asking people for the last five years. The fact is that people are generally unable to answer it until they have learned a new language, a new set of concepts and notions about thinking. That is what this chapter is about.

Perception

Let's first back up a bit, and look for a moment at an issue that is even more basic than ways of thinking.

The human eye is an amazingly complex mechanism. It is made up of cells, rods, pigments, nerve connectors, fluids, an incredible number of moving parts. The normal human eye is capable of perceiving several million variations of color, when it is functioning properly. The range of color discrimination between different sets of eyes is tremendous. Some people see little or no variation in color. Other eyes have discriminating ability to almost an infinite number of gradations. There are enormous variations in depth perception, in the ability to differentiate among textures, in peripheral vision, in perception of movement, in distant vision, in the ability to see patterns, in the discrimination of closeup details, in variations within and between areas of light and dark.

No two pairs of human eyes are the same, mechanically or anatomically. No two pairs of eyes see things in the same way. Our differences in perception begin with this basic and astonishing fact.

Even before we talk about learning, values, inferences, interpretations, attitudes, neurological differences or Styles of Thinking, we are confronted with this profound problem, relative to our ever being able to agree on anything. For each of us, even before the brain and our thought processes go to work, the world is a different place. Our differences in Styles of Thinking compound the complexity of the situation.

"Thinking × 5"

At the beginning of Chapter I, we said that most people are either one-way or two-way thinkers. But in our Western world, there are five distinct approaches to thinking, five distinct sets of cognitive strategies which people learn as they grow. Each has its strengths, each its liabilities.

Half of us tend to rely on a single set of strategies, with an intensity that ranges from a moderate preference for the single approach to a virtual commitment to it. Another 35 percent of us rely on a combination of two of the five approaches.

Our preferences for one or more sets of thinking strategies dictate our approach to problems, and to a great extent our behavior generally. Our preferences form the basis of our unique ability to handle tough problems and to meet the requirements of specific situations. They also lead us to mistakes and incompetence when the preferred approach doesn't work.

The technical name for the five approaches is *Inquiry Modes*:

that is, ways of looking at the world, making sense of it, and asking questions. For our purposes in this book, we prefer the term *Styles of Thinking.*

Certainly, one can say that there are as many ways of thinking as there are people, and one would be right to say so. But thinking behavior can be categorized. That is, although there are individual differences within each category, those who have a preference for a particular Style of Thinking tend to do many of the same things.

The five Styles of Thinking that we will discuss in this chapter and later make up a manageable set of categories. The categories derive from recognizable and accepted notions in Western history, philosophy, and methodology. Best of all, they can be measured with a reasonable degree of precision, and they can be tested and validated by the individual.

Before we talk about the five Styles of Thinking, it is time for you to take a look at your own preferences. Please turn to the back of the book, where you will find the I_nQ questionnaire.* Do the following:

1. Read the instructions carefully.
2. Fill out the sample question, and check back to make sure you have followed the instructions, and that they are clear to you.
3. Fill out the questionnaire, completing all the items. Take your time. Do it thoughtfully, and as honestly as you can.
4. Complete the score sheet.
5. Transfer your total scores to the five boxes which you will see at the top of the next page.

Once you have done all of this, we will move on to an explanation and interpretation of the five Styles of Thinking. You will have your own I_nQ profile to refer to. We can't think of a better way to understand thinking than to have your own way of thinking to think about.

Please go ahead with the questionnaire on pages 183–89.

Now, take your total scores from the large boxes at the bottom

* The i_nQ questionnaire is copyrighted (1977, 1980) by Bramson, Parlette, Harrison and Associates and reprinted by permission. For further information on its use in training, selection and group development write to BPHA, 2140 Shattuck Avenue, Suite 1210, Berkeley, CA 94704.

of the score sheet and post them here (or if you don't like to mark up a book, post them on a separate sheet of paper for easy reference):

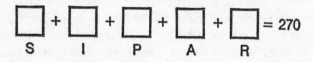

$$\square + \square + \square + \square + \square = 270$$
$$\text{S} \qquad \text{I} \qquad \text{P} \qquad \text{A} \qquad \text{R}$$

Your five scores should add up to a total of 270 points. If they don't, go back and check your horizontal and vertical arithmetic. Also, make sure you responded each time with a 5 for MOST LIKE YOU and a 1 for LEAST LIKE YOU.

Here are the names that have been given to the five Styles of Thinking, arranged in the order of the boxes on the score sheet:

Synthesist
Idealist
Pragmatist
Analyst
Realist

The words are fairly common, but we will be using them in particular ways, so don't take them yet at face value.

Before we talk about the Styles of Thinking, we need to explain something about the meaning of the scores in the "total" boxes.

Scores and What They Mean

If you have a score of 60 or more in any of the Styles of Thinking, you have a *moderate preference* for that Style (or Styles). That is, all other things being equal, your tendency will be to use that Style more than the others.

If you have a score of 66 or more, you have a *strong preference* for that Style. That is, you are likely to use that Style consistently and in most situations. You may occasionally overuse it or use it where it may not be the best approach, especially under stress. If you have a score of 72 or more, you have a very strong preference, or a *commitment*, to that Style. That is, you are likely to use that Style in virtually all situations, and you may frequently overuse it, or use it in situations where it may not be the best approach.

Now, of course, if you have one, two, or more high scores, you will have one or more low scores. If your score in any Style is 48 or less, you have a *moderate disregard* for that Style. If you have a score of 42 or less, you have a *strong disregard* for that Style. And if your score is 36 or less, you show a virtual *neglect* of that Style. That is, you are not likely to use it in any situation, even though it may be the best one to use under the circumstances.

Your high scores show you where your preferences lie. These high-scoring Styles of Thinking are your strengths. They indicate the kinds of thinking strategies you have learned and which you prefer to use, because they have worked for you over time.

Where a score is very high (approaching or over 70), it may be an indication of a problem for you. You may overuse your strengths, or use them inappropriately at times. In that case, *your strength becomes a liability*, and that is something to be aware of; and maybe to be wary of.

For many people, their lowest scores on the I_nQ are useful pieces of information. These scores can suggest to you where your weaknesses lie. Low scores indicate areas of strategy and skill that may be underdeveloped, underused, perhaps even ignored. As you go through this book, if you pay particular attention to those Styles of Thinking in which your score is low, and work toward learning the strategies and skills that go along with them, you can gain a great deal of benefit.

Some Notes on Interpretation

If the difference between any two scores is less than 4 points, you should assume that the difference is too small to matter. Suppose your I_nQ profile looks like this:

$$\boxed{45} + \boxed{67} + \boxed{51} + \boxed{64} + \boxed{43} = 270$$

$$\quad S \qquad I \qquad P \qquad A \qquad R$$

If you have a profile like this, you have an equal preference for the Idealist and Analyst Styles of Thinking. You are an Idealist-Analyst (IA). You will use those two Styles, most of the time in combination, and in most situations. If you look at the low scores, you will see what amounts to an equally strong *disregard* for the

Synthesist (S) and Realist (R) approaches. Under most circumstances, you will not use the S or R strategies, even though one or the other might be the most appropriate for the situation.

Suppose you have a measurable preference (a score of 60 or more) for a *single* Style of Thinking. If that is the case with your I_nQ profile, then you are typical of about half the people who have taken the questionnaire.

You may have scores of 60 or more in each of *two* Styles of Thinking. If so, you are typical of about 35 percent of the people who have taken the I_nQ. Any combination is possible, though some are more common than others, as we shall see later.

Only about 2 percent of all people who have taken the questionnaire show a 60+ preference for *three* Styles in combination. Again, any combination is possible, but if you have such a "three-pronged" combination you are a relatively rare bird.

What if you have a "flat" profile? Suppose you have no scores approaching either 60 or 48, but all are somewhere in the 50s. In that case, you have no strong preference for any particular Style of Thinking. If this is so in your case, you are typical of about 13 percent of all the people who have taken the I_nQ.

Now we will take a look at each of the five Styles of Thinking, in a sort of nutshell description. In Chapters III through VII, we will show how each of the Styles works in real life—how you know it when you see it, and the strategies common to each. Chapter VIII will explain and illustrate the different combinations, including the "flat" profile.

The Synthesist

Only about 11 percent of the people who have taken the I_nQ show a preference for the Synthesist Style. It is the least frequently found of the five Styles of Thinking. If your score here is not very high compared to the other four scores, you are in good company—about 89 percent of everyone you are likely to meet or work with. If you are a strong Synthesist, you have reason to believe that you are in a fairly select group, statistically speaking.

To "synthesize" means, essentially, to make something new and original out of things that, by themselves, seem very different from each other. Combining different things—especially ideas—in that way is what Synthesists like to do. Their favorite thought process is likely to be *speculative.* "What if we were to take this idea and that idea and put them together? What would we have?" The motto of the Synthesist is "What if . . . ?"

Synthesists are *integrators.* They like to discover two or more things that to other people may appear to have little or no relationship, and find ways to fit them into a new, creative combination. Synthesists aren't particularly interested in compromise, consensus, or agreement on the "best" solution to a problem. What they look for, instead, is some perspective that will produce a "best fit" solution, linking the seemingly contradictory views.

Synthesists work this way because they assume that no two people are likely to agree about "facts." Facts to them are not nearly so important as the *inferences* that people make from them. Unlike the other Styles of Thinking, Synthesists know that people really do disagree about the facts. And that, for Synthesists, is one fact that makes life exciting.

Synthesists tend to be interested in conflict. A strong Synthesist thrives on it, in fact. The kind of conflict that Synthesists enjoy may not be overt, open conflict such as a shouting argument. It may be more subtle than that: the enjoyment of listening to people talking politely, for instance, who assume they agree. The clever Synthesist, however, sees that they really do have differences, points them out, and then comes up with a new and original idea that builds on the differences.

Synthesists also like change—often for its own sake. Synthesists tend to see the world as constantly changing, and they welcome that view. For that reason, nothing bores the Synthesist more than the status quo, things never changing, routine, people always agreeing, or pretending to agree.

Synthesists are forever looking for conflict, disagreement, change, newness, and they have a habit of questioning people's basic assumptions about things. They pride themselves on their "creativity," incisiveness, and, often secretly, on their cleverness.

The Idealist

If your i_nQ profile shows a score of 60 or more in the Idealist Style, you are in good company. At least in our society, it is the most "popular" of the five Styles. More than 37 percent of all the people who have taken the I_nQ have Idealist preferences.

Idealists are people who like to take a broad view of things. They also tend to be future-oriented and to think about goals: that is, "Where are we going and why?" Because of that, Idealists are likely to pay attention to the needs of people, to what's good for them. They often think about things by asking what they are good for in terms of people or society. This is especially true when there are problems to be solved or decisions to be made. In other words, they are interested in social *values*.

Idealists are like Synthesists in their focus on values rather than facts. The difference is that while Synthesists assume that no two persons will agree on the facts, and therefore solutions to problems will come from creating something new to integrate opposing views, Idealists take a quite different approach. Idealists also understand that people differ, but they like to believe that arguments and differences can be *reconciled* by emphasizing the similarities that can be found even in opposing views. Idealists believe that people will agree about anything once they agree on goals. Unlike Synthesists, then, Idealists don't value and enjoy conflict. It seems nonproductive and unnecessary to them.

Idealists like to be seen by other people as helpful, supportive, open, trustworthy, and useful. They tend to have a strong ethical sense. Their philosophy of life will often sound something like this: "If I am a good person and do the right thing, I will get my just rewards."

Idealists pride themselves on their high standards, though they are not always aware of just how high their standards are. They want high quality in work and social affairs. Idealists are often especially interested in "quality of life" and what's good for people and for society as a whole. Because of their high standards, Idealists are often disappointed in others whose aspirations seem less lofty. They can become angry at and resentful of those who seem to care little for others, who lack integrity, or who will settle for less than the best.

The thought processes of Idealists are *receptive*. They welcome a diversity of views. When there is a problem to be solved or a decision to be made, they welcome a broad range of views and many alternatives. What they want to do then is to *assimilate* all those views and alternatives, and come up with a solution that will have something in it for everyone. The symbol of Idealist solutions might be the *umbrella:* a solution that will be comprehensive and pleasing to all involved. Committed Idealists can sound as if they are seeking Utopia.

When it comes to problem solving, Idealists are at their best in situations where the important things are values, judgments, feelings, and emotions, the subjective factors in the situation. Neither the Synthesist nor the Idealist approach is at its best when the problem to be solved is one that is well-formulated, structured, and can be calculated, "figured out" logically, or put in mathematical terms. Idealists especially pride themselves on their "intuition."

The Pragmatist

We have found a preference for the Pragmatist orientation in about 18 percent of the people who have taken the I_nQ, which makes it, next to the Synthesist, the second least "popular" Style of Thinking. Thus, if you are a strong Pragmatist, at least four out of five people you deal with are likely to find your style confusing, difficult, or at least "different."

The motto of the Pragmatist is: "Whatever works." They verify what is true or false in terms of immediate personal experience. This gives them a freedom from consistency that lends itself to experimentation and innovation. Pragmatists excel at finding new ways of doing things with the materials that lie at hand. They tend to approach problems in a piecemeal, incremental fashion, one thing at a time. They are interested in "getting from here to there," in making do, and in looking for the shortcut and the quick payoff. They have less interest in the "big picture" and high standards of the Idealist, or the logical, planned, well thought-out approach of the Analyst.

In their concern for "workability" as the test for usefulness, they resemble Realists more than any other Style of Thinking.

To others, the approach of the Pragmatist may appear superficial, lacking in standards, erratic, and even irrational. Pragmatists, to other people, often appear short on convictions or consistency.

But somewhere deep in the mind and the value system of the Pragmatist is a conviction that is very firmly held. The Pragmatist is convinced that, in this world, things really do happen in a piece-meal way, one thing at a time. While the Analyst believes in predictability and the Idealist in a "grand design," the Pragmatist believes in nothing of the kind. The world is neither predictable nor capable of being understood, much less managed, as a whole.

Pragmatists tend to be less predictable than people who prefer other Styles of Thinking. Facts and values have equal weight for them. Again, "whatever works" is what is important. Subjective factors such as emotions and feelings become facts for the Pragmatist, if they are relevant to the situation.

Pragmatists are apt to be interested in formulating strategies and tactics for getting things done. They have a grasp of what people will buy, and what will sell.

Pragmatists often like to be liked, approved of, or at least accepted. They tend to show well-developed social skills. They are good at putting themselves in other people's shoes, and have a sense of both the practical and the human impacts of a proposed decision. In other words, the Pragmatist approach is flexible and *adaptive*. And Pragmatists take pride in their adaptability.

The Analyst

Analysts approach problems in a careful, logical, methodical way, paying great attention to details. Planning carefully, they gather as much information as possible before making a decision, and they seldom "shoot from the hip." If your Analyst score is 60 or more, you are in almost as numerous a company as the Idealist. About 35 percent of all the people who have taken the I_nQ show a high Analyst score.

When we have talked about the Analyst Style of Thinking in seminars, Analysts themselves are often surprised—and sometimes offended—when we say that the Analyst is more interested in "theory" than the other Styles of Thinking. Strong Analysts see themselves as factual, down-to-earth, practical people, and of course in a sense they are. But beneath the attention they give to facts there are broad and deep theories.

Analysts tend to have a theory about almost everything. They analyze and judge things within a broad framework that will help to explain things and arrive at conclusions. For example, if we were to ask an Analyst whether or not a park should be built in such-and-such an area of his or her city, the reply will follow the gathering of data and the weighing of alternatives. What the Analyst is likely to be unaware of is that the kind of data gathered and the way the alternatives are weighed will depend upon a deeply ingrained theory of government. If the theory is, "The function of government is to do as little as possible," only the strongest of "Yes" facts will get much attention. If the Analyst believes that, "The function of government is to do as much as possible," the answer will be quite different.

The Analyst sees the world as logical, rational, ordered (or orderly), and predictable. Or, if that worldview is impossible to sustain because of current circumstances—say there is rioting in the streets—somewhere deep in the Analyst's value system is a belief that at least the world *ought* to be that way.

The Analyst's thought processes are *prescriptive*. When a problem is presented, the Analyst will look for a method, a formula, a procedure, or a system that can solve it. Because of their interest in formula and method, Analysts like to find the "one best way" to solve a problem. Of all the Styles of Thinking, they are likely to say: "If we can only proceed in a scientific manner, things will work out."

You can see how different the Analyst approach is from the other Styles of Thinking we have looked at so far. While the Synthesist is interested in conflict, change, and newness, the Analyst prefers rationality, stability, and predictability. Where the Idealist is focused on values, goals, and the "big picture," the Analyst prefers to concentrate on objective data, procedure, and the best method. If the Pragmatist's approach is piecemeal and experimental, the Analyst's is quite the opposite: planned out and based on finding the proven "one best way."

More than anything else, Analysts want to be sure of things, to know what's going to happen next. They take pride in their competence, in the sense of understanding all the facets of whatever the situation in which they happen to be.

The Realist

When we come to this fifth Style of Thinking, we have come a long way from our starting point, the Synthesist. The Realist is in most respects at the opposite end of the thinking spectrum from the Synthesist. If you have a high Realist score, you are among the 24 percent of people who share that preference.

Many people who hear us refer to Realists and Pragmatists as different say, in effect, "Why, they're the same thing." Indeed, the two terms are often used interchangeably or synonymously. After you have read this section, go back and compare it with our description of the Pragmatist. You will see that although there are similarities, the two are different enough to be considered quite distinct Styles of Thinking. They rest on different assumptions and values, and the strategies used, while often complementary, are also quite different.

Realists are empiricists. That is, what is "real" to them is what can be felt, smelled, touched, seen, heard, personally observed or experienced. The Realist's motto is, "Facts are facts." Or maybe, "What you see is what you get." The Realist is contrary, in this respect, to the Synthesist, who, you will recall, assumes that inferences, rather than perceived "facts," are all-important.

While the Synthesist firmly believes that agreement and consensus are most unlikely to happen between people in a given situation, the Realist just as firmly believes that any two intelligent people, properly equipped with eyes and other sense organs, will at once agree on the facts. Therefore, agreement and consensus are most important and highly valued by the Realist. But being a Realist, of course, he or she can see quite clearly that people *don't* always agree on the facts. And that is exactly what bothers the Realist, because people *ought* to agree.

Without agreement on the facts, Realists believe, things don't get done. Things don't get *fixed*—and Realists value that word in both senses: to correct problems, and to make solutions last and stay put. The Realist's thought processes, then, have a *corrective* quality. Realists see something that is wrong—a problem—and they want to fix it. They are oriented toward achieving concrete results. Unlike Pragmatists with their experimental tendencies,

Realists want to do things surely, soundly, and firmly, and to be assured that once something is done it will stay that way.

The Realist is more closely related to the Analyst than to any other Style of Thinking. Both are factual, oriented toward the objective and concrete, interested in an orderly and practical result. Both share an antipathy for the subjective and the "irrational." Where they differ is that the Realist will grow impatient with the deductive, drawn-out procedures of the Analyst. The Realist wants to get things done by proceeding on the facts that are at hand, rather than by gathering ever more data, as Analysts like to do. The Realist is inductive and empirical, the Analyst is deductive and analytical.

Curiously, while Synthesists and Realists are at opposite ends of the Style of Thinking spectrum in many respects, they may behave in similar ways. Both can be seen as people with a need to achieve, to move, to be in control. Simply stated, Realists need to control resources, people, and results; while the Synthesist's need is for control over the *process*—understanding and staying one step ahead of the argument, the conflict, the decision.

Both the Synthesist and the Realist tend to become easily impatient, especially with excessive analysis and long-drawn-out, rambling discussion. Both pride themselves on their incisiveness, and both can be incisive, sometimes disturbingly (or annoyingly) so. The difference is in the nature of their favorite incisive questions. The Synthesist asks: "What are the basic assumptions in this situation?" But the Realist asks: "What are the facts?"

Looking Ahead

We have explained the basic notion of Styles of Thinking. You have had a chance to take a measurement of your own preferences in strategic thinking. If you are like half the people who have taken the I_nQ, and have a single strong Style of Thinking preference, chances are this brief nutshell description has given you some insight into your own Style. It may have given you some ideas about just how different other people are from you in their approach to problems and decisions.

What we have tried to do here is give some idea of what it's like to have a preference for each of the Styles of Thinking. In the next chapters we are going to look in more detail at each of the five Styles, at their strengths and liabilities, and especially at the strategies common to each. Later we will share some ideas about how to acquire and develop the strategies that can broaden your own thinking repertoire.

Chapter III

THE STRANGE WAYS OF SYNTHESISTS

How to Know a Synthesist When You See One

Synthesists are apt to appear challenging, skeptical, or satirically amused, even when you can see no cause for any of that. They like to express concepts rather than specifics; they can appear out of touch with concrete reality. They are prone to expressing opposite points of view, especially to what is popular or upon which everyone else seems to agree.

Besides their enjoyment of speculation, Synthesists like to point out the absurdities in a situation. "Look at us. Here we are busily planning next year's budget, and the whole company might go out of business tomorrow." Sometimes they just don't seem to take things as seriously as others of us would like.

Synthesists enjoy speculative, philosophical, intellectual argument, so long as it doesn't get too somber and the silliness of the act of argument itself is acknowledged. They are apt to use parenthetical expressions, qualifying adjectives and phrases— especially words like "essentially," "primarily," "more or less," "relatively." They engage in digressions that sometimes seem to have no relevance to the matter at hand. But if you listen carefully, they usually have relevance, though you may have to grope for it.

Synthesists dislike talk that seems simplistic, superficially polite, fact-centered, repetitive, or "mundane." They may or may not be "deep thinkers," but they often sound that way. Sometimes they sound as if they think they know the secrets of the universe. The next minute what they are saying sounds just silly. And here is one almost sure clue: When you hear someone expressing a well-argued, philosophical, profound idea, and then the person suddenly breaks off and pokes fun at his or her very own idea, you know you are hearing a Synthesist.

The strategies favored by Synthesists can add an enormous amount to the richness and variety of anyone's thinking. Synthesists themselves can be exciting people to have around, but for almost nine out of ten of us, our first problem with Synthesists is Synthesists themselves. They are "different."

Synthesist Grand Strategy: The Dialectic

A good part of that differentness comes from the grand strategy of the Synthesist—the Dialectic. In formal academic terms, the dialectical approach to knowledge rests on these three elements:

Thesis—that which already exists, or which is known, accepted, generally believed.

Antithesis—what is new in the world, just emerging and becoming known, not yet accepted, and which challenges popular belief.

Synthesis—the new, original, "creative" result of the integration of the thesis and antithesis.

The dialectical approach assumes that the thesis and the antithesis are in conflict. It also assumes that conflict is a creative process. In our society, conflict is not generally accepted in that way, nor is the dialectic itself a generally accepted mode of inquiry.

Thus we can see why Synthesists might appear "different" from the start. While the particular Synthesist of your acquaintance may not be consciously aware that he or she uses an approach formally known as the dialectic, nevertheless that is the foundation of that person's way of asking questions and solving problems.

All of the Synthesist's specific strategies, which we will look at now, are variations on the dialectical theme.

Synthesist Strategy #1: Open Argument and Confrontation

The Synthesist isn't at all averse to direct confrontation, for the purpose of having disagreement acknowledged and dealt with. Even if the Synthesist is personally one of the two sides of the argument, that presents no difficulty. Though it's usually more fun to be a third party while someone else fights.

Here is an example. Warren is often retained by companies as a trainer for the purpose of helping to build a coordinated, harmonious executive team. The process that he uses works something like this:

Warren meets separately with individual executives. He gathers confidential information from each one about things that are going well in the company and things that aren't going well. Typically, a good deal of the information is about other executives who are doing things that the person interviewed thinks are nonproductive or worse.

Warren then has a meeting of the whole group. There, he "feeds back" the information he gathered during the interviews. The intent is for the group to acknowledge and identify the problems that have emerged from the interviews. With Warren's help, they then try to find ways to solve some of the problems.

Even though any number of interpersonal conflicts clearly showed up in the interviews, it frequently happens that the group shies away from dealing with them in open forum. Warren, a confirmed Synthesist, is convinced that such "personality" issues are among the most important in an executive team, and that they must be dealt with if the team is to work effectively.

After a time, if the group continues to avoid talking about its interpersonal problems, Warren will try this technique. First, he seats the members of the team in a circle, so they can all see each other. Then he says: "I am going to count out loud to three. When I say 'Three' I want each of you to point to the person in this room who gives you the most problems."

Sometimes, of course, people will still refuse to participate. Hands remain clenched in laps, index fingers twitching. But when the experiment works, it works dramatically. It is certainly a way to get a conversation started. And that is all that Warren wants to happen.

This rather daring technique stems from a basic Synthesist assumption: that conflict is bound to be present in a given situation, so why not bring it out and deal with it? And because of that assumption, and perhaps their need for achievement, Synthesists will often become impatient with a drawn-out process, and have at it as soon as possible. Why not? the Synthesist thinks. It's bound to come out in time.

To others, the approach can seem aggressive or abrasive, even destructive. To the Synthesist, it's just a matter of common sense, of the way the world is. The strategy consists of voicing all sides of the argument, and in that way confronting it. A vital part of the Synthesist Style of Thinking is to *feel* the reality of all the conflicting viewpoints.

Synthesist Strategy #2: Asking Dumb-Smart Questions

Keith Peters is a computer expert who markets software and programming to various companies. Let's tune in, for a moment, to his conversation with a new client, an executive vice-president of an insurance company.

> CLIENT: Well, Mr. Peters, now that you've had a chance to look over our data processing system, I assume you're in a position to say how you might help us.
>
> KEITH: I might be. What did you have in mind by way of help?
>
> CLIENT: Well, in my opinion, we're strong in the Claims and Underwriting areas. Our data bases are very good there. What I had in mind was our Actuarial data base. And Investments too. We don't seem to get timely information in either area. Any ideas?
>
> KEITH: Sure. You don't need timely Actuarial information. You need good, accurate projections, that's all. And you don't need computer software for that. All you need is a couple more good technical assistants to the Actuary, with a pair of high-speed calculators.
>
> CLIENT: Oh, really!
>
> KEITH: Right. And your basic problem with investments is that your Investment Officer isn't on top of things. All he needs to do is get to work two hours earlier, so that he's in touch with the East Coast market on time. You have more basic problems than that.
>
> CLIENT: We have?
>
> KEITH: You said your Claims data base is sound?

CLIENT: I did.

KEITH: It depends on what you want to get out of it. Right now, all you have is a fancy accounting system. I think you need more sophisticated information than you're getting.

CLIENT: Can you help with that?

KEITH: Not yet. You have still a more basic problem.

CLIENT: What, for heaven's sake?

KEITH: Your present data processing staff isn't capable of designing a basic Claims system, much less new, sophisticated data bases.

CLIENT: So what do I do?

KEITH: Beef up the staff, and bring in a heavy training program. After that, we might be able to help you.

CLIENT: Look, this isn't what we called you in for.

KEITH: What's your basic business?

CLIENT: Why, selling insurance, of course.

KEITH: Wrong. Your basic business is moving money. You're losing a great deal of money in Claims. And you can't correct that until your systems people are competent enough to give you proper information.

In Keith's case, of course, whether or not he gets the contract depends on the client. A client who can survive having his basic assumptions called into question, who can tolerate being told that he is looking into the wrong problem, who can adjust to flat-out disagreement, might award the contract to someone like Keith Peters, other things being equal. But for many, it's a bit hard to take.

Synthesist Strategy #3: Participating from the Sidelines

This strategy demands a special skill, which can be learned, and seems to come more naturally to Synthesists than to other people.

Perhaps it is because Synthesists tend to be "outsiders" (remember, they are only 11 percent of us). Participating from the Sidelines, also known as third-party observation, means to be part of the action, but above it or outside it at the same time. The key questions are: "What's going on here?" and "What part am I playing in this?"

Arbitrators, judges, statesmen, college presidents, and city managers need to develop Synthesist skills, because strategies such as this one are essential to their roles and their performance.

The third-party tendency can be a source of great discomfort to Synthesists if it is not understood. It is not comfortable, after all, always to feel something of an outsider. But once the tendency is understood, and developed as a skill and a purposeful strategy, it becomes very powerful.

Therapists, ministers, marriage counselors must cultivate the skill. To the extent that they are comfortable with the Synthesist orientation they are likely to be that much more successful and less emotionally stressed from their connection with the torn lives of others. The strategy requires the ability to observe, to make inferences about what lies beneath superficial behavior, to feed back what has been observed without judging or condemning, and in that way to help people get fresh insights into what they are doing. It also requires a good deal of strength and emotional stamina, because that kind of feedback isn't terribly welcome for many people.

We can't see ourselves in action, after all, as well as someone else can. If we are genuinely interested in knowing how others see us, a skilled Synthesist may be the best person to ask.

Synthesist Strategy #4: Suspending Opposing Ideas

The novelist F. Scott Fitzgerald once wrote: "The ability to hold two opposing ideas in the mind and suspend them there without becoming confused, is the mark of a mature intelligence."

Whether that judgment is true or not, Fitzgerald spoke of a typical Synthesist strategy. A Synthesist finds it enjoyable to entertain entirely opposed ideas while waiting for a resolution to "come" intuitively, or to emerge from the conflict, while others are likely to be confused or tired out by the same process. Opposing ideas are the raw materials of synthesis, of the dialectical process which is the Synthesist Grand Strategy.

A hospital administrator, for instance, sits in on an argument among the staff over budget cuts. The director of nursing says, "Cutting my budget makes no sense. The goal of this hospital is to provide the best possible care to our patients, regardless of the cost." The director of finance says, "Not so. Our goal is to stay financially viable so that we can remain in business and provide a service to the community."

The Synthesist administrator knows that both viewpoints are true (or maybe both are false; that is beside the point), and deliberately suspends judgment. The administrator's skill will be demonstrated if an *integration* of the two opposing ideas can be found which will allow both sides to be heard but still keep the hospital functioning.

Here is a description of the Synthesist approach to knowledge by the British philosopher, Sir Stuart Hampshire:

> I have looked in philosophy, as also in fiction and poetry, not for a greater clarity in familiar ways of thought, but rather for a particular kind of confusion. The confusion is that which comes from trying conflicting possibilities of description, and from postponing a decision between them. It is the kind of confusion that occurs when one listens to different voices speaking different languages at the same time, and when one will not stop one's ears against all the voices other than the most familiar ones.[1]

Synthesist Strategy #5: Speculation and Fantasy

We said earlier that speculation is a tendency of the Synthesist. It can also be a deliberate strategy, the key question being, "What if . . . ?" "What if we let Johnny have his own car, even though he's never taken care of anything in his life?" "What if we threw out all the computers?" "What if we decided to move to Montana and start a magazine?"

The Synthesist regards questions like these as creative. They can open up new horizons, stimulate thinking. Committed Synthesists find that they have to be careful with the strategy. It needs to be used judiciously. In many situations to other people, it can sound silly, irrelevant, frivolous. "We're dealing with *facts* here, not speculation!" To some people it can be maddening, anxiety-raising, especially if the Synthesist is the boss.

[1] Stuart Hampshire, *Modern Writers and Other Essays* (New York: Knopf, 1970).

We once worked with a large regional planning agency, where a new executive director had recently taken over. The executive director, Terry Sandoz, was young, energetic, curious, and given to the speculative habit of saying, "What if . . . ?" For his staff, Terry proved to be something of a problem. Every time he said "What if . . . ?" someone ran off to start a new project.

The director of planning would call in one of his division heads. "Terry wants a study done on the feasibility of merging the police and fire departments of Lake Villa and Franklin Woods." The division head would hold an emergency meeting of his staff. "Hold everything. We have a new project." Six people would go to work fulltime for a month gathering data, analyzing, writing a report, compiling tables. The report would come back three times from the director of planning, wanting more details.

Finally the report reaches Terry. "What's this for?" he asks. The director of planning reminds him that he requested the study. "I did? When?" He is reminded of the date and circumstances.

"For heaven's sake," Terry says. "You and I were talking about the general subject of public safety consolidation, and I happened to be looking at a map. All I said was, 'What if Lake Villa and Franklin Woods were to consolidate?' It just jumped out at me from the map. I was only speculating. I didn't mean a formal study to be done!"

Meanwhile the same sort of thing was going on all over the agency, with staff members complaining that priorities were constantly changing because of Terry's "demands." At last, it took a retreat by Terry and his senior staff meeting with a full-scale staff before people began to understand that Terry loved to say "What if . . . ?" He was not issuing commands. Once people began to understand that, some of them even came to enjoy it.

Synthesist Strategy #6: Proposing "Far-Out" Solutions

William J. J. Gordon, in his book *Synectics*, which is about creative problem solving, shows how "play and irrelevance" can be important elements of an original solution. In one of our favorite passages from his book, a group of problem solvers has been assigned the task of designing a container that will dispense everything from glue to nail polish. To work well: the opening of the container must close tightly and cleanly after each use. Here is the end of the problem-solving conversation:

> D: When I was a kid I grew up on a farm. I used to drive a hayrack behind a pair of draft horses. When a horse would take a crap, just his outer . . . I guess you'd call it a kind of mouth, would open. Then the anal sphincter would dilate and a horseball would come out. Afterwards, everything would close up again. The whole picture would be clean as a whistle. . . .
>
> B: You're describing a plastic motion.
>
> D: I guess so. . . . Could we simulate the horse's ass in plastic?[2]

This is a fine example of problem-solving playfulness strategy that Synthesists tend to enjoy thoroughly. But, as with speculation, Synthesists find they have to be judicious with its use. Most people, when they have a problem to solve, are very serious about it. Synthesists who are too free with their tendencies are apt to find themselves thrown out of the room.

Synthesist Strategy #7: Negative Analysis

This is a most valuable strategy, one that we believe should be cultivated by more people, especially in organizational decision making. It would save so much time, trouble, and money if, after an important decision has been reached, someone were to say: "What will go wrong if we go ahead with this?"

The trouble is, many people find such questions annoying, if not downright rude and disruptive. Idealists, for instance, want to have everyone rally around their decisions, because now everything is going to be all right and everyone is going to be happy and work together toward implementation. Realists hear such questions as disputatious, arbitrarily questioning the facts and threatening the consensus that they value so highly. Analysts, as

[2] William J. J. Gordon, *Synectics: The Development of Creative Capacity*, (Macmillan, 1961), p. 43.

careful, thoughtful planners, object to such questions as irrelevant: "Haven't we already covered all the contingencies in our plan?"

Psychologist Jerry Harvey wrote an article for the *Harvard Business Review* a number of years ago called "The Abilene Paradox." Here is a summary of his story.

> Harvey and his wife were visiting his in-laws at their house in a small town about sixty miles from Abilene. It was a hot summer day, and to keep cool they spent a pleasant afternoon playing dominoes and sipping lemonade on a shaded patio.
>
> Late in the afternoon someone (no one was ever quite sure who) said, "What do you think about going to Abilene for dinner?"
>
> Someone else said, "Why not?"
>
> Another said, "Sounds okay to me." Before long they were all in the car on their way to Abilene.
>
> It turned out to be a hot, miserable drive to the city. The family had a dinner that wasn't very good. After another long, hot ride they all arrived home tired and out of sorts.
>
> "Whose idea was that, anyway?" someone said.
>
> "I thought it was yours."
>
> "Well, I was only making a suggestion."
>
> "I said yes only because I thought it was something *you* wanted to do."
>
> They discovered that no one had really wanted to go to Abilene. But they all went and had a miserable time because no one took the risk of going beneath superficial politeness and assumed agreement to point out why the trip might not be a good idea.[3]

Harvey uses this anecdote as an example of what happens to many people, groups, and organizations because of similar behavior. The trip to Abilene was an example of "groupthink," the phenomenon of everyone going along because no one wants to seem "negative." People keep their thoughts to themselves: "Everyone

[3] Adapted from Jerry Harvey, "The Abilene Paradox," *Organizational Dynamics*, Summer 1974, pp. 63–80.

else seems happy about it—there must be something wrong with me." Yet, under the circumstances, some form of devil's advocacy may be exactly what is needed.

Devil's advocates are not well received by many people. They can sound to others like negativists. Yet the strategy of negative analysis can be of enormous value in helping to prevent bad decisions. It is a special strategy of Synthesists, but unfortunately one that they often find themselves having to suppress, in order not to be seen as troublemakers.

The Strengths and Liabilities of Synthesists

Let's return to Keith Peters, the marketing director for a computer software firm. He is a brilliant man, as everyone says who knows him. As a computer expert, he excels at those brilliant flashes of insight which characterize what we know of the creative genius. He can put ideas together in original combinations that would seldom occur to other people. His success in marketing is a result of those skills: in a remarkably short time, he can look over a customer's data processing system, think about it from several different points of view, and quickly "see" what needs to be done. Clients are most impressed with his ability (though some are scared off by it), and business is thriving.

A few years ago, when Keith was working in Boston, he needed a home for his family. He traveled to the suburb of Marblehead, famous for its Colonial houses, fell in love with a great, rambling old home, and bought it. It was just too unusual for Keith to pass up. His house had six bathrooms, and every weekend it seemed another toilet was out of order, another hot-water shower outlet leaked. Those problems were symptomatic of the house as a whole. It was a venerable, romantic, rundown mess. It would have been ideal for a person with the time, motivation, and skill to restore it. But Keith was a busy man during the week, and he treasured his weekends for relaxation and his hobby, sailing. The house at Marblehead turned out to be a disaster for him.

Keith Peters is a Synthesist thinker. It is the Synthesist quality of mind that produces those penetrating and unusual solutions to problems. It is also what makes Keith seem something of an oddball to his friends and some of his clients. Synthesists are capable of truly exciting mental gymnastics, because they are willing to look at things from odd points of view. They can perform astounding achievements because they are open to ideas that to other people might seem "far out" or absurd. In other words, they are willing to take substantial risks in their thinking.

But that same ability causes them sometimes to make personal decisions that bring them grief. That is because of their attraction to the strange, the unusual, and the new, and their lack of attention to the mundane, the ordinary, and the details of things—such as the bathrooms in Marblehead.

Synthesists tend to be people who believe they have important things to say. They find it stressful and even threatening when they feel they aren't being listened to. Then they are likely to "act out," often by using their style unproductively—inappropriate humor, irrational playfulness, pointed satire and sarcasm. When a Synthesist comes across as a troublemaker, it is usually because his or her intellectual pride and authority aren't being properly stroked.

Because Synthesists are so interested in conflict, disagreement, and the process by which such differences take place, they often appear lacking in personal commitment. A common Synthesist liability is a lack of follow-through and attention to the details of carrying out a decision. That is because, once a decision is made, a problem solved, or a conflict resolved, the situation is no longer of interest to Synthesists. They would prefer to go off and find a new conflict. They have a way of remaining uninvolved, of being able to stand back and say, "Isn't that interesting?" while everyone else is emotionally overloaded.

The strength-liability paradox of the Synthesist can be summed up like this. When Synthesists make a right decision, the result can appear an act of brilliance. When they make a wrong one, it can be catastrophic, because it is so far off the mark.

Or to put it another way: Don't look to a Synthesist for caution or moderation. They like to do things in a big way or not at all.

Chapter IV

THE WHOLESOME WAYS OF IDEALISTS

How to Know an Idealist When You See One

Idealists look and respond attentively and receptively. They show a supportive, open smile. They do a good deal of head-nodding. They give verbal and nonverbal feedback that serves to encourage you to be open with them, to trust them, to see them as helpful and receptive. They may not be aggressive in offering their own ideas and opinions, but they listen and they welcome yours.

Idealists are apt to express their feelings, their values, their ideas about what's good for people, the community, society. They express concern about goals and the long-range aspects of things.

The tone of Idealists tends to be hopeful and inquiring. They ask a lot of questions, but sometimes their questions sound tentative, even apologetic. They don't like to step on other people's toes, or to sound challenging. Above all, they are uncomfortable with conflict or open argument. They want people to agree, and to be "nice" to each other, and they often will show, in their openness and receptivity, a strong tendency to trust others, sometimes more than is wise.

Idealists enjoy feeling-level discussions about people and their problems, and abstract discussions about philosophy and ethics—so long as the discussion does not become acrimonious. They dislike talk that seems data-bound, too heavily factual, or "dehumanizing." They hate openly conflictual argument.

Idealist Grand Strategy: Assimilative Thinking

"Wholesomeness," then, has two meanings in terms of the Idealist. The one we are concerned with here is the one that can be defined as the assimilative approach. It rests on two basic Idealist assumptions.

The first assumption is that the world can be a better place, and people can live together in it harmoniously, if only they can agree on overall goals. That is, the Idealist believes that disagreement and differences can be assimilated and harmonized.

The second is what we might call the "holistic" assumption. Everything is connected with everything else. In order to understand any problem, we need to look at the total context. It is another form of assimilation, in which we try to look at the relationships of things and events with a broad perspective.

Some form of assimilative thinking seems to characterize most Idealist thinking processes. Hence we can call it the Idealist Grand Strategy. All of the specific Idealist strategies flow from that source.

Idealist Strategy #1: Focus on the Whole

Here is a dialogue involving the supervisor of a secretarial pool and two clerks.

> SUPERVISOR: I'd like your opinions about the new invoice form from the Planning Department—the one for consumable supplies. Have you had a chance to look at it? What do you think?
>
> ADELE: Well, it looks pretty simple and straightforward to me. It's no more work for us than the old one. Just the boxes are in a little different arrangement.
>
> SUPERVISOR: What do you think we need to do?
>
> ADELE: Not much. A half-hour orientation session for the pool should do it to train them.
>
> SUPERVISOR: Jerry, what do you think?
>
> JERRY: Well, there are a couple of things I'm a trifle concerned about.

SUPERVISOR: Yes?

JERRY: For one thing, it looks almost identical now to the form for nonconsumables. I'm afraid the order clerks in the departments might find it confusing. Errors could be made, don't you think?

SUPERVISOR: I see. Good point.

JERRY: And while it's no more work for us, it seems to me that the form requires more information than is really needed. Especially the parts that the clerks in Supply have to complete. I'm afraid they'll feel overloaded.

SUPERVISOR: Well, that's fine, Jerry, but is all that really our concern?

JERRY (apologetically): Maybe not. But I'm just thinking about the company as a whole.

Jerry's point is that in order to understand the pros and cons of the new form, it needs to be looked at in a total context. When Idealists talk this way they are worth listening to. By looking at the whole, thinking about relationships, being concerned about the feelings of others, they can force us to focus on the real impact of our decisions and actions. A simple form can look like merely a simple form to the rest of us. In a complex organization that simple form can have all sorts of ramifications. In order to understand them, the problem has to be looked at in a broad context.

Idealist Strategy #2: The Long-Range View

Several years ago, we were asked to help with the merger of two community volunteer groups, who wanted to join together in order to establish an agency that would have more clout and better financing than the two separate agencies of the past. Both were rural groups, that had traditionally and geographically been separated by a range of mountains.

We worked with the two groups to help them set goals, develop policy, and build an organizational structure. Meanwhile the young executive director, who saw a successful merger as his primary responsibility, was especially careful about one thing. On either side of the mountain was a large county town. Each of the former agencies had its own board, a separate staff, long-standing regional allegiances. The executive director understood that the question of where the new joint agency's headquarters would be was an important question as well as a potentially explosive one.

In leading the planning meetings of the two boards, our friend carefully kept the groups focused on the long-range issues, and convinced them not to look at the "headquarters" question until the very end of the process. Once the organizational structure was set, by-laws agreed upon, and all the volunteers had actually merged, *then* the headquarters site was decided on—logically and easily, as it turned out. By then everyone was so committed to the organization and its goals that the headquarters question had become a relatively unimportant, routine one.

It is exactly over such "practical" questions as that of headquarters in this example, that so many decision-making groups are thrown off the track and prevented from going where they really want to go. The executive director of the merging agencies was primarily concerned about the long-range good of the organization and the total community. He used all his influence and persuasive powers to make that a common focus—and the results were successful.

Idealist Strategy #3: Setting Goals and Standards

Working with problem-solving and decision-making groups, we constantly observe a pair of phenomena that have been given these names:[1]

Rush to Structure. This happens when someone in the group takes the initiative and says, "Well, how do we go about this task?" and then he or she gets the group organized, decides the best way to proceed, and works out a plan. What isn't done is to take the time to decide just what the task is, where the group wants to end up, and what alternative approaches might be available.

Preemptive Participation. The minute the group gets settled (or sometimes even before that), someone says, "Let's get on with it." Someone else says, "Here's what we'll do," and then the next

[1] We owe these terms to Raymond E. Miles of the University of California, Berkeley.

thing you know the group is rushing busily ahead—somewhere. It all depends on who says what first. Again, no one takes the time to talk about "What?" "Why?" "How?" Two weeks later, the group pulls up short when some Idealist finally speaks up and says, "Wait a minute, please. Are we going where we really need to go?"

One frequent and enduring problem for Idealists is their reluctance to use their valuable strategies forthrightly. They don't like conflict and disagreement. They avoid confrontation, thus they avoid the kind of assertiveness in a group that might prevent Rush to Structure or Preemptive Participation. It is an irony. Idealists want not to be seen as challenging or nonsupportive, so they avoid doing exactly what, in the long run, would be most supportive for the group, which is to help set goals and establish standards.

Idealist Strategy #4: Receptive Listening

Receptivity comes naturally to Idealists. They understand intuitively that there are many possible solutions to a problem, and many satisfactory alternative courses of action in any situation.

It is when Idealists learn to use their natural receptivity as a purposeful strategy that they begin to use their strengths productively. Once that is understood and utilized, a number of skills begin to emerge:

—Idealists tend to be better *listeners* than the rest of us. They are more open, patient, tolerant of differences. Their natural quality of being nonjudgmental can become *empathy*. They can develop a real ability to understand the views of others, even when they may not agree with them.

—Because they are receptive and listen well, Idealists can be very good at *gathering information*. So long as they can remain relatively objective, they can learn, more easily than others, not to screen out data. If they cultivate the skill, they can improve their decision-making powers simply by drawing upon a broader base of information.

—Idealists, as managers, supervisors, group leaders, can use their receptive skills to build group involvement, to increase *participation*. They tend naturally to be drawn to a participative approach, and their strengths tend to be perfect for it. They learn to make sure all the members have a chance to be heard, that all ideas are considered, and that everyone has a voice in decisions.

The problem with all this, for Idealists, is that their very receptivity draws out and encourages conflict and differences of opinion, and that is worrisome for them. But to make up for that, another Idealist strategy proves to be immensely valuable.

Idealist Strategy #5: Search for Aids to Agreement

Life is a constant process of influencing others. We are forever engaged in trying to get others to agree with us. But "influencing," for many Idealists, is something of a bad word. It suggests a certain imposition or manipulation (and the latter is a *very* bad word to Idealists). The most important thing, for Idealists, is to help or to "facilitate" agreement between people. So their strategy consists of looking for aids to agreement.

One of the favorite aids is to draw a picture. The picture might look something like this, on the first try:

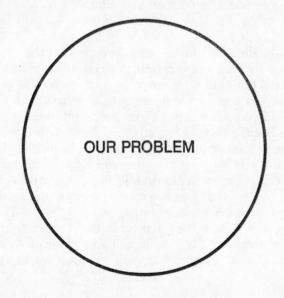

Then the next draft might look like this:

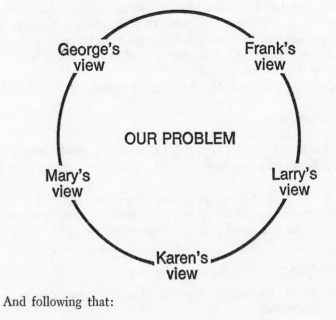

And following that:

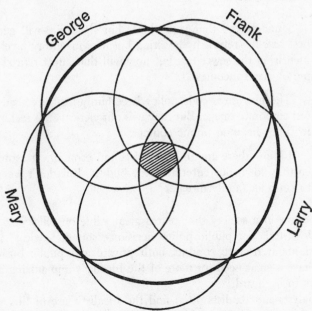

Then the Idealist leader says something like this: "You see, though we have five differing views, they all have a few things in common. See how they overlap? Now, can we talk about what's in the area of overlap? What are the areas of the problem where we all agree? Let's work on that."

Other aids that Idealists like to use are verbal; expressions such as:

"It seems to me. . . ."

"George, don't you think that . . . ?"

"I thought I heard Larry and Karen saying much the same thing, though they may have sounded very different. Here's what I heard. . . ."

A special Idealist aid to agreement sounds something like this: "Now I'm sure we will all agree that we have the same basic purpose. Can we talk about that and then get to the specifics?"

Idealist Strategy #6: Humanizing the Argument

The use of this strategy depends on asking appropriate questions, such as these:

"I understand that your chart shows the city will get the best revenue return by lowering business inventory taxes and increasing the sewer tax, but how will that affect retired people on fixed incomes?"

"The new dress code policy is certainly logical considering our corporate image. But how will our clerical staff feel about it? They have no public contact."

"I know there are all kinds of sound economic reasons for cutting down our entertainment budget. But don't we need to consider family morale?"

We live in a society that places great value on efficiency, economic criteria for public policy decisions, sound, "logical" judgments about how to conduct both private and public business. We have a great need for more of the Idealist's humanizing arguments to be heard.

Analysts and Realists often find the Idealist's use of this strategy annoying or downright irrelevant. Especially so when they can clearly see that the situation at hand is objective, clear, and can be logically or factually "calculated out." Synthesists and Pragmatists sometimes find it simply boring, when overused. For Idealists, on the other hand, Humanizing the Argument is not only right and proper. It is a moral and ethical imperative.

Idealist Strengths and Liabilities

Jane, a social work supervisor with twenty years' experience in community agencies, tells of a problem she has with her younger caseworkers. The conversation goes something like this:

JANE: I can't seem to convince them to do the job properly.

WE: They aren't performing?

JANE: Oh, they work hard. I can't say they're not performing.

WE: But they cause you problems anyway.

JANE: It's their attitude. They bring up all these ideas about casework that just aren't right.

WE: Such as?

JANE: Well, I was trained to practice nondirective counseling methods. Clients should be given the chance to work out their own problems. Caseworkers are there to help them do that.

WE: But your younger people do it differently.

JANE: Sometimes I can't believe what I hear. They act like Dutch uncles. They will *tell* a client what to do.

WE: Do they do it all the time?

JANE: Oh no. Just now and then.

WE: Do they get results?

JANE: Well, yes. For the short run, anyhow. But I wonder sometimes about the long-range effect on the client.

WE (persisting): But the results they get are generally satisfactory? They meet agency standards?

JANE: Mm—yes. I can't really criticize them for that. But I just wish they would do it the *right* way.

Jane was trained in an idealistic, supportive casework method. Her younger employees sometimes take a more pragmatic or realistic, direct approach. Jane's training and her preferred way of thinking about casework (and probably about many other things in her life) make it difficult for her to acknowledge that anyone could succeed as a caseworker using another set of strategies.

At the heart of Jane's problem is a commitment not only to a certain method and approach, but to a set of basic values. The method and the values go hand in hand. In effect, they define Jane as a professional. She is uncomfortable when others use methods different from her own, because that is a violation of her value system. To the extent that others succeed while using such methods, Jane's discomfort is increased.

Notice, that is true of all of us. The importance of the individual value system as one determinant of behavior and attitude is not peculiar to Idealists, such as Jane. What is peculiar is the *weight* given by Idealists to their values, to value judgments, to moral questions, and ethical principles.

Because of all that, Idealists are more prone than others to experiencing *dilemmas*. They often find themselves in situations where either of two choices is equally unsatisfactory. Because Idealists want to do the "right" thing, in terms of their high standards and values, and because they are so receptive to differing views about how things should be done, they tend to suffer about decisions more than the rest of us do. Their decision processes are internal and subjective. They aren't likely to ask objective questions, such as "What works?" or "What's been proved?" Instead, they are constantly asking, "What's *right*?"

That is why Idealists, overusing their strengths, are so often called "bleeding hearts" by other people. Take the director of nursing in a community hospital, Marcia G., who agonizes because she knows some patients aren't getting the best possible care. She is deeply disappointed because some of her nurses are more interested in pay and hours than in the patients. They aren't idealistic enough, the way nurses ought to be.

Marcia lectures her nurses in a motherly way, she pleads with them, she appeals to their high standards, but to no avail. Told by outside observers that there are some simple things she might do by way of a better scheduling and supervisory system that would save money and give her nurses more time to devote to patients, Marcia rejects the suggestion.

"System" is irrelevant to her, if not a bad word. What is important is people. They *ought* to work hard. They *ought* to be motivated. Doesn't Marcia herself work twelve hours a day, six days a week? She does that because it is *right* to give and to be dedicated. If others did as she does, everything would be just fine.

Idealists reject other approaches for different reasons. They reject the Pragmatist approach because it seems so superficial and expedient. They reject the Analyst approach because it is dehumanizing. They reject the Realist approach because it is hardheaded. They find the Synthesist approach uncomfortable and just plain "not nice," because it is based on conflict and because Synthesist solutions don't really "solve" anything. The Idealist wants everyone to be satisfied.

Idealists, being supportive, receptive people, often seem self-effacing too. Frequently, while he or she works hard to facilitate agreement among other people, the Idealist's own views are either absent or tentative. That is a typical Idealist problem. When they leave themselves out of the action in their desire to facilitate agreement, sometimes the decision that is reached turns out to be the "wrong" one; one which doesn't meet the Idealist's own high standards. When that happens, Idealists suffer.

Sometimes Idealists nurse their resentment and disappointment indefinitely, rather than go against the group. If the result of the decision goes awry later, they may have a strong tendency to say, "I told you so." Then, of course, they want to be helpful and supportive toward getting things back on the right track.

All of these characteristics make up the "wholesome" ways of Idealists. Idealist ways are wholesome in the best sense, because they are based on high standards, on moral and ethical values. And Idealists are wholesome in the sense that they look at what they believe is the "whole" of the situation. They find it difficult to understand people who don't operate in the same way.

The most serious Idealist liability derives precisely from the Idealist's greatest strength—reliance on high standards. A typical Idealist blind spot is an inability to recognize just how high those standards are. Sometimes Idealists' standards are set so high that they themselves can't live up to them, not to mention other people. So Idealists tend to suffer two related pangs—guilt over disappointment in themselves, and hurt feelings over disappointment in others.

Idealists are wholesome people, and we need to nurture them, just as they feel a need to nurture us. Like anything wholesome, they are good for us, in the proper proportions. And in the case of Idealists themselves, their valuable strategies also need to be used in the right proportions.

Chapter V

THE PIECEMEAL WAYS OF PRAGMATISTS

How to Know a Pragmatist When You See One

Like the Idealist, the Pragmatist often has an open, sociable appearance, but in a way that is more mercurial, less intense, and perhaps more spirited than that of the Idealist. Pragmatists often show a good deal of humor, a quickness to agree with others' ideas. "I'll buy that," they say. "That sounds pretty good to me."

They enjoy light social interplay. They tend to be enthusiastic and agreeable; though sometimes they overdo it to the point where they sound insincere. They like to be liked, but in that respect they tend to take themselves and the relationship not quite so seriously as do other people. "Well, if she doesn't like me, I'll just try someone else."

Pragmatists enjoy lively give-and-take, brainstorming, clever conversation, and lighthearted scheming, especially on tactical issues. Like Synthesists, they enjoy playing with ideas, though usually at a less philosophical, more down-to-earth level. They dislike talk that seems dry, dull, or humorless. They clash with Synthesists over talk that seems too conceptual, abstract, or speculative. They grow easily bored with discussion that seems too analytical or nit-picking.

In short, Pragmatists are often good people to have around. Their enthusiasm and experimentalism tend to liven things. In problem-solving and decision-making situations their skills can be immensely valuable, if they can be properly utilized. What that means is: Pragmatists have to be given room, loose reins, and to be kept interested. Once you have allowed Pragmatists to become bored, you have lost them.

Pragmatist Grand Strategy: The Contingency Approach

What is the contingency approach?

Very simply, it is an overall strategy based on two closely related principles: "Whatever works"; and "It all depends on the situation." What others—especially Analysts and Idealists—find hard to understand is that the contingency approach is not simply random behavior, a reactive process of response and adaptation, but a deliberate, purposeful strategy when it is exercised by Pragmatists who know what they are doing.

"It all depends."

"Whatever works."

"One thing at a time."

The contingency approach is the Pragmatist's "theory." It is also a "contextual" theory. That is, the contingency approach says that a problem or a decision is looked at in the context of the situation at hand.

Where the theory falls down is in this respect: only the individual, the actor, can determine what the context of the situation is. It is purely a matter of judgment at the moment. The Pragmatist assumes that there are *no rules* for the process of judging the nature of the situation or its context. One does not look at the big picture, the grand design, or the logical structure of the situation. One simply *apprehends* and *experiences*.

To that, Analysts and Idealists are apt to say, "Well, how then do you ever *know* anything?"

To which the Pragmatist is likely to respond, with an amused grin, "You *don't* ever know." And that, for Pragmatists, is part of the joy and challenge of life.

We can call the contingency approach, then, the Grand Strategy of the Pragmatist. Other Pragmatist strategies are very much in tune with that overall notion. Let's look now at a few of them.

Pragmatist Strategy #1: Moving One Step at a Time

The technical name for this strategy is *incrementalism*. It is also known as the *piecemeal* approach. It comes from one of the most basic Pragmatist assumptions—that the world is itself a piecemeal affair. Though we may talk about goals and whole systems and long-range plans, the fact is, for the Pragmatist, that such things are only words and phrases, at best general guidelines. The way things really happen is one step at a time.

Two important areas of human activity come to mind when we think of incrementalism: international diplomacy and economic development in less-developed countries.

While they may often have some kind of grand design in mind, successful diplomats treat such images only as hypotheses or "what-ifs." While the goal may be, for instance, peace in the Middle East, such apparently aimless activity as "shuttle diplomacy" seeks to get a tentative agreement here, a compromise there. To the extent that each step-by-step agreement or compromise can help to achieve a goal, to the diplomat that's just fine. But one can be satisfied with an increment. Next time around, perhaps another one. Accomplished diplomats must have a strong pragmatic bias. Otherwise they are likely to become, at best, highly frustrated.

Orderly, planned, long-range economic development can take place only where there is already a strong economic base, a stable infrastructure. Until those foundations are established, a developing country has to build itself incrementally: a dam here, a factory there, a hospital over there—when they can be afforded. Leaders in less-developed countries have to be accomplished and deliberate Pragmatists in order to survive.

Curiously, though we Americans have always thought ourselves as pragmatic, much of our technical assistance to developing countries has been based on Analyst and Idealist assumptions and strategies, which almost always have failed. It is only in recent years that we have discovered the piecemeal nature of economic development in such places. For instance, we have funded the construction of great factories in India and East Africa, without paying attention to basic needs for the training and even the nutrition of those who might operate the plants. We have encouraged and supported massive programs of birth control without understanding that basic religious and social attitudes toward child-bearing need to be changed before birth control programs can work.

The Peace Corps and VISTA, for instance, seem to be founded on a Pragmatist, "whatever works," piecemeal philosophy. We suspect that those volunteers who don't make it are those who can't handle the ambiguity of their work.

Pragmatist Strategy #2: Experiment and Innovation

Ambiguity is an important word to remember when we talk about Pragmatists. Of all the five Styles of Thinking taken singly, that of the Pragmatist has the highest tolerance for ambiguity. That is, Pragmatists have less need than the rest of us to know exactly where they are going, to understand precisely what is happening around them, or to have a sense of predictability about events.

It is exactly their high tolerance for ambiguity that leads Pragmatists to be interested in experiment and innovation, to try things out in order to see what will happen. The strategy, after all, is a means for coping with ambiguity. Once you have completed a successful experiment, and it works, then you *know* something you didn't know before. If you can't know anything for sure, or in advance, as Pragmatists are likely to believe, the strategy makes perfect sense.

Innovation means, most simply, to do something new and better than before with the materials at hand—whether those materials are things, people, or ideas. The innovator introduces a change by making something new and different. With such an interest and tendency, the Pragmatist resembles the Synthesist. The difference is this: Synthesists have a tendency to look for change for its own sake, from boredom with the status quo and to satisfy their "creative" needs. Pragmatists look for change for practical (or "pragmatic") reasons. The Synthesist wants something new and profound. The Pragmatist simply wants a payoff.

Pragmatist Strategy #3: Looking for Quick Payoff

It is probably this Pragmatist strategy that has the most usefulness in organizations and groups. Pragmatists, understanding and using the strategy purposefully, can have incredible value to an organization, when the strategy is used appropriately, and when it is seen by others as "okay." The basis of the Quick Payoff strategy is an acknowledgment that the environment is constantly changing, so that it is necessary to *adapt* to it.

Here are Del and June Robertson. They are nearing fifty, and have always dreamed of having a retirement home of their own in northern Wisconsin. Once a month for years they have driven from their home in a Chicago suburb to the Rhinelander-Eagle River area to look at real estate. Every year, for their vacation, they rent a different nearby cottage for a sizable sum. Yet, they never seem to discover the "right" place.

As Idealist-Analysts, Del and June pursue a steady, prudent course toward a goal that keeps receding into the horizon. While they have almost $30,000 in savings, inflation keeps driving the cost of property higher at twice the rate they are saving. Their retirement home account grows but its buying power evaporates as they search for just the right place.

If only Del and June were Pragmatists. They would invest that money in property that isn't quite "right," improve it, and turn it over. Step by step, proceeding that way, they might come closer to their ideal, and turn a profit while doing so. As Pragmatists, Del and June would pay more attention to the Quick Payoff, and could be better off for doing so.

Pragmatist Strategy #4: Tactical Thinking

Picture a smoke-filled room. We are in a city of fifty thousand citizens, where a group of people from the same part of town have come together to plan a political campaign. They want to elect a slate of candidates to the city council, so that certain programs which they all support will get funded. Here is a portion of their conversation.

BILL: The question is, how do we get three or four people elected, in different districts, when almost no one knows who we are or what we advocate?

SHIRLEY: It seems to me that we have to educate the public. If they don't know what we believe in, how can we expect them to vote for it?

ED: That's right. We need a massive publicity campaign. Ads in the newspaper, spots on TV, posters all over town.

BILL: That's going to take a lot of money, which we haven't got.

JEAN: Look, there are ten of us, right? If we all go out and call on people, that's only—

BILL: With twenty thousand households in town, that's two thousand apiece. Sounds unrealistic to me.

SHIRLEY: How about a sound truck? If we have a good message, we can take it all over town, relatively cheaply.

ED: How much money do you think we ought to have, to successfully elect three people?

BILL: About fifty times more than we've got.

JEAN: Oh, it all sounds so hopeless!

RAY: Wait a minute. Maybe we ought to look at it another way.

ED: How's that?

RAY: Maybe we just elect one person, someone from our district. If we concentrate on that, we should be able to pull it off.

SHIRLEY: But we have to have more clout than that.

RAY: Okay. Maybe we can educate a few of the incumbent councillors. Who do we know that might support us, if we could get to them?

ED: Maybe Smith, and Ellis. Maybe Gonzales.

JEAN: And perhaps Truesdale, though I'm not sure.

RAY: Well, with one of our own people on the council, that makes five. And that's a majority.

BILL: How do we go about it, Ray?

RAY: Which of those people do any of us know? (Silence.) Okay, who do we know who knows any of them?

SHIRLEY: My best friend lives next door to Councillor Truesdale, though I've never met him.

ED: My sister-in-law is a cousin of Councillor Smith's husband. And both of them are close to Ellis.

BILL: Hey! Come to think of it, my dentist plays golf with Gonzales every week.

RAY: It sounds as if we might be on our way. Let's start making the contacts and getting to know those people.

It is in just such a way that many real-life political changes have taken place. Ray understands perfectly that politics is "the art of the possible." His Pragmatist approach has helped this group lower its sights from the level of grand strategy and wishful thinking to what is do-able, considering the group's resources. His tactical thinking has brought them to a point where they can do something specific.

Tactical Thinking is first cousin to the strategy of One Step at a Time. It is an important part of the art of the Pragmatist.

Pragmatist Strategy #5: The Marketing Approach

A word of caution to Idealists.

The next time you hear someone say "But will it *sell?*" when you are preoccupied with all of the social benefits of the idea that is under discussion, don't dismiss the question as superficial or cynical, much as you may be tempted to do so. Listen to that Pragmatist talking. He or she may have something important to say.

The conscious cultivation of the Marketing Approach is rarely more practical than in the matter of applying for a grant, a frequent activity these days among individuals and community groups. Typically, a group applies for a grant from the government or a foundation with the most laudable of aims. The purpose for which the money is to be used is a noble one. The group may be able to articulate its objectives clearly, and may show evidence of good planning and fiscal management skills.

But then the group asks for the moon, and rests its case on the intrinsic goodness of the cause. "If they can't see how worthwhile a proposal this is, then we don't want their money." It is likely to be an "all or nothing" approach.

What is needed are some good Pragmatist questions:

—Who is our audience?
—What kinds of things are being funded these days?
—If we can't get all the money we want, how much are we willing to settle for?
—What's the best way to package our proposal?
—Who do we know who can help us sell it?

So many plans and good ideas go awry because they fail to sell. So many well-meaning people find their projects going down the drain because no one will buy them. The "all or nothing" strategy rarely works in the real world, which after all, like it or not, is to a large extent a market. As those who have cultivated the strategy know, the Marketing Approach can not only be useful toward achieving more important goals, it can even be fun.

Pragmatist Strategy #6: Contingency Planning

Skillful Pragmatists are seldom caught in the trap that is so familiar to many of us—seeing their projects fail, and experiencing despair because with the project everything else seems to have gone down, too. Pragmatists seldom go bankrupt, because they don't put all their eggs in one basket. In their incremental, experimental, playful way, Pragmatists like to have any number of projects going at once. If two or three of them fail, it's not overall disaster, and there is always something else to do that is interesting.

Similarly, a typical Pragmatist question is, "If this goes wrong, then what do we do?" But this "analyzing" strategy is quite different from that of the Analyst. For the Analyst the question is, "If something goes wrong at this point, how do we correct it to get back on track?" For the Pragmatist the question becomes, "If something goes wrong at this point, what other tracks might we take?" The Pragmatist is not concerned with the "one best way." He or she knows there isn't such a thing.

One of the greatest strengths of contingency planning, as practiced by Pragmatists, is a willingness to cut losses. Unlike the rest of us, who doggedly plod ahead with our projects because so much time and effort has already been invested, the Pragmatist is always prepared for the basic contingency:

"Well, that didn't work out. Let's try something else."

Pragmatist Strengths and Liabilities

Peter S. is the city manager of a medium-sized city on the West Coast. He has been in that position for eight years. Seen by many others in his field as an energetic, intelligent, and unorthodox fellow, he has acquired a national reputation as an innovator in city management. Peter is considered to have advanced ideas, to be knowledgeable academically, but more impressively, he has actually tried to practice many advanced notions. He has experimented in his city—sometimes successfully, sometimes not—with any number of new organizational management methods and techniques.

While he is admired by "progressive" people in his city, Peter's reputation within the organization is decidedly a mixed one. A number of the city council members are displeased with him. They see him as restless, unpredictable, impulsive, and hard to control. There is a sizable element of the city staff in which there is active dislike, not so much of Peter himself as of his management practices.

Peter is said to keep people off balance, to lack structure or visible direction, to be inconsistent between authoritarianism and participation, to engage in "seat of the pants" management. Some people express exasperation with Peter's insistence on "it all depends" as his guiding principle. They see it as a non-principle. Almost all of the senior managers who were in office when Peter took over have either left the city or have taken an early retirement, in reaction to Peter's management approach.

Here is another example of a Pragmatist in action. By his late forties, Richard Noonan had experienced considerable success as vice-president and treasurer of a large manufacturing concern. He had also been active for years as a trustee of the small liberal arts college from which he had graduated.

Noonan was an expert in finance, with particular skills in managing investment programs. He had made a great deal of money for his company by the shrewd investment of funds for high return and short-range payoff, within the framework of a flexible overall investment plan.

When he decided to retire early from the company, Noonan tried to become a consultant to privately endowed colleges. He offered to manage their investment programs for them, in order to improve their generally shaky financial condition. There was no doubt that Noonan had something to offer his potential clients which could be of great value to them. What went wrong had to do with his approach. Here are his words:

> "These boards of trustees are all very conservative and idealistic. They think only about the long run, their obligation to society, the quality of their curriculum, and all that sort of thing. They are afraid of experimenting, of playing with their investment portfolios so as to get a quick return. In my opinion, that is exactly what they need, and of course it's what I've been trying to sell them. I urge them to diversify and experiment, but they simply won't listen to me."

After two years of frustration, Noonan gave up his practice and returned to a fulltime job. The most competent of experts in his field, he had failed to adapt to the thinking of his potential clients. His experimental, quick-payoff approach scared off the very people he wanted to serve. He was unable or unwilling to adjust his style to people who valued idealism, long-range stability, and endurance.

A major liability of Pragmatists, then, derives from their very adaptability, and their paradoxical failure to see that others aren't as adaptable as they are. Others need structure, a plan, predictability, long-range goals. Pragmatists, the most adaptable of people, often fail to adapt productively to others, thus losing the payoff of their greatest strength.

Chapter VI

THE ORDERLY WAYS OF ANALYSTS

How to Know an Analyst When You See One

For many of us, the initial impression made by Analysts can pose a problem. They tend to appear cool, studious, perhaps distant, and hard to read. Conversing with Analysts can be difficult, especially if you happen to be trying to sell them something. There may be a lack of feedback, as if they are hearing you out (they are!). Idealists particularly, with their constant need to communicate and be in touch, find that characteristic disconcerting.

Analysts are easy to identify in casual conversation. Listen:

"It stands to reason . . ."

"If you look at it logically . . ."

And of course:

"If we just go about it scientifically . . ."

Analysts are apt to express general rules, more or less precise "theories" about things. They describe things systematically and carefully. Analysts are those people who will often tell you more about something than you really wanted to know.

Their tone is likely to be dry, disciplined, and careful. Under stress, they are apt to sound set and stubborn. When you push Analysts too far, they will simply withdraw. They may not leave the room and go home to their stamp collections; they simply withdraw on the spot. It is as if a curtain drops behind their eyeballs—a Great Stone Face waiting it out until there is someone sensible to talk to.

Analysts enjoy structured, rational examinations of substantive issues. Other things being equal, for instance, they are more likely to enjoy a formal lecture on some subject of importance than something like group encounter. They use long, discursive, well-formulated sentences. They dislike talk that seems irrational, aimless, or too speculative and "far out." They tend to dislike irrelevant humor.

The great cross that Analysts have to bear is that, to others, they often seem unemotional and lacking in a sense of humor. On that score we would say that Analysts are probably more private and selective with their emotions than other people, but not necessarily less emotional. And the Analyst's sense of humor can be delightful. It is apt to be subtle, dry, and witty in a special way. The Analyst's sense of humor is often hard to get to, but the work involved can be more than worthwhile. Lovers of Lewis Carroll and "Monty Python's Flying Circus," for instance, know that. Analyst humor is often based on rational premises carried to their utmost logical absurdity.

Many connoisseurs have strong Analyst proclivities. They approach nothing lightly, but thoroughly and studiously. Thus, it would take a knowledgeable Analyst to inform us of the relative worth of a hundred fine wines, and to let us know that "technically," rosé is only to be drunk with peanut butter sandwiches.

Analyst Grand Strategy: Search for the One Best Way

Let's look briefly at the steps by which Analysts usually pursue their search:

1. Gather data, in order to:

2. Define the problem thoroughly and accurately, followed by:

3. Search for alternative solutions, which are to be evaluated against:

4. A set of specific decision or selection criteria, leading to:

5. Selection of the best alternative, after which decision we:

6. Implement the solution; which does not end the process, because finally we must:

7. Evaluate the outcome of the solution to make sure it was really the one best alternative.

And if our solution does not, in fact, turn out to be the best one, we start the process all over again.

The method is clear-cut, it is founded on formal logic, and it is "analytical" in the true sense. That is, it seeks to break the situation down into its component parts, to define a problem by isolating it, and to make it manageable in that manner.

Where the Analyst Grand Strategy goes wrong is when it is seen as the *only* method—which, unfortunately, is the most common error that Analysts make. Let us look at the favorite strategies of Analysts to see why that might be so, and to understand the power of those strategies.

Analyst Strategy #1: Systematic Analysis of Alternatives

To look at this strategy, let us choose a homely example—planning a trip.

Imagine that you have a new job, and you are going to move your household in a rented truck from Syracuse, New York, to Pittsburgh, Pennsylvania. You look over the roadmap, and see that there are three apparently reasonable routes that you could choose:

—The most direct route seems to be toward the southwest, on a series of secondary roads.

—You could drive west to Buffalo, then southwest to Erie, south from there to Pittsburgh, with the whole trip done on freeways.

—You could drive south to Harrisburg, also on a freeway, then catch the Pennsylvania Turnpike directly west into Pittsburgh.

All three routes seem logical, so in order to choose between them you must gather more data. Your next step is to compute the actual roadmap mileage for each alternative.

You are somewhat surprised to find that what had appeared the most direct route—the first alternative—turns out to be almost as many road miles as the other two. Those secondary roads wind all over the hills of western New York and Pennsylvania. You further consider the fact that you will be driving a heavy truck, with which you haven't had much experience. Driving on those narrow roads will be hazardous at worst, exhausting at best. So you reject the first alternative.

You compare the remaining choices, and find that the mileage is almost the same for each. You are attracted to the southern route, via Harrisburg, because it appears less congested than the western route which just bypasses the big cities of Buffalo and Erie. But, for more information, you call the state highway police, and they inform you that, at the time your trip is planned, the freeway between Scranton and Wilkes-Barre will be closed, resulting in a long detour. Further, you discover that the Pennsylvania Turnpike toll for your big truck will be quite large. Finally, your wife remembers that she has a cousin in Fredonia, New York, with whom you could stay at no cost, halfway along the Buffalo-Erie route. Your choice is made. Not, however, by hunch or impulse of the moment, certainly not in a hurry.

When you arrive in Pittsburgh safe and relatively fresh after two trouble-free days, you pride yourself that an analysis had in fact given you the one best way to go. For you know that, simple as the process was, most people wouldn't have bothered with it. The Realists and Pragmatists would simply have loaded their trucks, glanced at the map, and started driving—into who knows what perils and difficulties.

So the strategy is immensely useful, when the situation can be calculated in a logical, analytical way. When that isn't so—especially in those cases where people hold different values, different views of the situation—the One Best Way strategy may not be the one best strategy to use.

Analyst Strategy #2: The Search for More Data

This is an admirable strategy, one that could be of great value to others if they could learn to cultivate it. It is really quite a simple approach, but Pragmatists and Realists, for instance, often find it too time-consuming. It seems to them like little more than a delaying tactic to getting on with the job.

Here is an example. We are sitting in on a meeting of several marketing experts in an electronics firm.

ELEANOR: All right, we're in agreement. The big push will be on the new microcomputer.

LOU: Right. And have we agreed that the primary target will be medium-sized firms on the West Coast?

JACK: Uh-huh. We'll get right onto the copy preparation with the advertising people. I'm thinking of full-page ads in the West Coast edition of *Business Week*.

ELEANOR: It's a heck of a market. I have visions of selling like hotcakes. What's your opinion, Elias?

ELIAS: Well—I have a couple of things I'd like us to think about.

JACK: What?

ELIAS: I'm all for the microcomputer. Don't misunderstand me, I think it's a great product. But I'm not sure about either the timing or the test market.

ELEANOR: What do you mean?

ELIAS: Let's assume the ads really work, and suddenly we have all sorts of inquiries and orders. Can we meet the demand?

LOU: Production says we can.

ELIAS: In my opinion, their estimates are fuzzy and overly optimistic. I'd like more data from them before we rush ahead.

ELEANOR: And what about the test market?

ELIAS: Well, why the West Coast? Our competitors are in that market pretty heavily. I'd like some more information about that, too. For instance, there might be real growth markets in places like Phoenix and Albuquerque. The advertising cost wouldn't be so great, and we might get a better feel for things there. I'd like to see us have preliminary studies there, and maybe in Atlanta too.

ELEANOR: Well, for heaven's sake, why didn't you say all this earlier, before we got so far down the road!

ELIAS: I've been sort of listening and thinking about it. Sometimes it takes awhile, you know.

There is no doubt that a person with Elias' Analyst tendencies and talents is a fine addition to this group. In fact, time may prove that he is indispensable to it. It is especially in enthusiastic, motivated, fast-moving groups that Analyst strategies are often needed. Someone like Elias, with his expressed need for more data, can provide a brake on movement that might otherwise be impetuous if not disastrous.

The difficulty for Analysts in such a situation is that, instead of being an appropriate and welcome brake, their strategy can look like a damper to others. When everyone is keyed up and ready to move, who wants to hear some wet blanket say, "Wait a minute. Do we really know enough about what we're doing?"

Like Idealists pleading for more attention to goals and high standards, Analysts often need to be more assertive in their request that we pay attention to details and constraints. They can both sound like voices crying in the wilderness, and they need to be listened to.

Analyst Strategy #3: Conservative Focusing

We have borrowed the name for this strategy from Robert V. Seymour* whose work contributed much to our understanding of human thinking. Conservative Focusing is a technical name for something that Analysts do almost as a matter of habit or instinct. Expressed simply, it means to isolate one variable at a time when looking at a problem. If that variable turns out to be the cause of the problem, then we have solved it. If not, we go back, isolate another variable, and start over.

For instance, suppose the electric dryer has stopped working for no apparent reason. For many of us, our first response will be to acknowledge our ignorance of appliances or electricity or both, throw up our hands, and call the repairman, at anywhere from fifteen to thirty dollars an hour. Not so for Analysts, whether they know anything about electrical appliances or not. One variable at a time, they proceed to analyze the problem.

Is there a fuse blown in the house system? That can be checked quickly. If not, is the appliance plugged in properly? Is the outlet

* Attributed to him in Jerome Bruner, et al., A Study of Thinking (New York: John Wiley and Sons, 1956).

working? Both of those items can be easily verified. Is all the wiring properly connected? We can take off the back plate and check that visually. If that produces nothing, how about the switch? It can be removed, taken down to a repair shop, and checked. What about the heat discs? The careful Analyst discovers there are two of them. They come out and go down to the repair shop. Usually, that is where the cause of the problem lies. A simple sixty-cent piece of equipment saves a thirty-dollar repair bill. Or, if that isn't the case, then a simple question at this point reveals that the motor must be burned out. Now the Analyst realizes there is big trouble, but at least the situation is clear.

Conservative Focusing is a strategy that could stand many non-Analysts in good stead. But it can be too time-consuming in many situations, and inappropriate in others.

Analyst Strategy #4: Charting the Situation

When the Executive Director of the East Liverpool United Fund has a problem or a major decision to make, she always draws a chart. First, she defines clearly, to her own satisfaction, exactly what decision she needs to make. Then, down one side of the chart, she lists all her objectives: that is, the things she *must* accomplish and the things that would be nice or desirable to accomplish by her decision. Then she puts values or *weights* on each objective—that is, numbers. In this way, her objectives become selection criteria, each of which has a different relative value for her.

Only now does the executive director list her possible solutions —the alternatives that might be available. Then, she evaluates each alternative, in turn, numerically against the value of each objective, adds the scores, and comes up with a "winning" choice.

This is one example of many approaches to decision making and problem solving which rely on Charting the Situation. It is a system of which Analysts are particularly fond, because it is a way of structuring a problem, of making all its components visible in order to analyze it, and of reaching an objective solution.

The great value of Charting the Situation is that it forces us to *display and array* the dimensions of our problem. This is something that intuitive people often fail to do, to their cost. Once

the dimensions of a problem are made visible, our focus is improved. We know more about the problem than we knew before. Sometimes the solution simply "jumps out" at us without the need for further analysis.

Analyst Strategy #5: Constructive Nit-picking

While Synthesists excel at what we have called Negative Analysis, Analysts employ a similar strategy—Constructive Nit-picking. It is a result of their skill in paying attention to details, their desire for thoroughness, their need for careful planning and well-built structure prior to action.

The Synthesist and Analyst strategies, while apparently similar, are very different. The Synthesist asks, "What might go wrong?" at a relatively high level of abstraction. Synthesists, in effect, are often questioning the whole concept under discussion, because they are so aware that a completely different concept might be just as workable.

Analysts come at their form of devil's advocacy from the opposite perspective. Having determined a One Best Way to proceed, they want to be sure it will work as planned. That is, they want a predictable, sure result, and their concern is that something might go wrong because an important detail has been overlooked. Analysts know that is how plans go awry. It is the little things, the details, that cause problems.

Analyst managers and supervisors often cause anguish to their subordinates by their nit-picking ways. The letter that is sent back three times for rewriting, the blueprint that is off by two scale inches at one corner, the account ledger that comes close but doesn't quite balance. "Picky-picky," the staff complains. "Why do we have to work for a perfectionist?"

Truly, the approach can easily be overdone. But there are situations where it is a vital necessity—*someone* has to look out for the details. For example, sometimes there is no surer way to lose a customer than to spell his or her name wrong in a letter. Errors of grammar or spelling in a publicity brochure are certain to present a non-professional appearance. Those of us who pay too little attention to details, but want to accomplish great things in the

community or the marketplace are often in dire need of a good nit-picker.

Analyst Strategy #6: Deductive Reasoning

Deduction is the act of proceeding from general principles to the understanding of specifics. As a strategy, it is what we spoke of earlier as the Analyst's "theoretical" approach. It is what Analysts naturally do and what often makes them powerful thinkers, leaders, and problem solvers.

Here is an example. George, a district sales supervisor, is complaining to his boss, Harry, the corporate sales manager, about one of his people.

GEORGE: Denny just isn't making it as a salesman. He looked so good when we hired him, but he's never met his goals yet.

HARRY: What seems to go wrong?

GEORGE: Beats me. He gets out and hustles, he makes a lot of calls, but he has a hard time closing a sale.

HARRY: Do you know why?

GEORGE: No, I sure don't.

HARRY: What is Denny like as a person?

GEORGE: Well, he's a nice guy. I mean a really nice guy. He's friendly and open and people like him. And he's always very helpful.

HARRY: What about the customers that he's managed to sell. Do they like him?

GEORGE: Oh yes. Very much. But a few of them have gone over to the competition.

HARRY: Why is that? Any clues?

GEORGE: Maybe. Several of them have said that when salesmen from the competition come in with a new product pitch, Denny has no good counterargument. It's as if he says something like, "Well, it's up to you, Mr. Customer."

HARRY: So he's not prepared?

GEORGE: Oh, I think he's prepared. It's more as if he just doesn't like to stand up and fight.

HARRY: George, what do we know about our competition's sales staff?

GEORGE: Aggressive as all get-out. They're in there fighting tooth and nail.

HARRY: And our own best people?

GEORGE: Same thing. Sometimes it's like a war out there.

HARRY: So what does that tell you about Denny?

GEORGE: Yeah, I think I see it now. He's in the wrong job, or at least the wrong market.

The deductive Analyst, like Harry in this example, can help us look at the problem from a different perspective. Analysts do this by trying to bring the focus to the level of theory. The key question is "What do we know about . . . ?" Instead of looking at an isolated instance, or a specific accident, we are obliged to start from a broader view.

Deductive Reasoning can lead to valuable insights that often can't be reached by any other method. It is a strategy which needn't be exclusive to Analysts. It can be learned.

Analyst Strengths and Liabilities

When Frank Daw became President of Tradesman's Industrial Liability and Casualty Company at the age of sixty-two, he was not at all surprised. It was only logical, he thought. Frank had been moving steadily along the path toward the executive suite ever since he joined the company as a junior accountant thirty-five years before.

Frank had never done anything but the right thing. Thorough and careful, highly responsible and dependable, Frank had always been the one whom more senior executives, as they rose and moved on, looked to when something needed doing that had to be done perfectly.

There was even a joke in the company along those lines. Frank Daw, it was said, had become president on the strength of his skill in writing reports. For at least thirty years, he had been the final authority on important reports to the insurance commissioner, and on the annual financial statement. If he didn't prepare the reports himself, he was always the last reviewer. He never missed the smallest discrepancy, and nothing ever went out of his office that wasn't perfect down to the last decimal point.

When he became president, Frank encountered two problems—though he never saw them as problems himself, only others did.

First, the president before him had been a completely different sort of person. Frank's predecessor had been known as a "mover and shaker," a lively, outgoing, innovative man who had brought about many changes in the company, who prided himself on his ability to inspire people and motivate them by his own spirited example. In contrast to the former president, Frank seemed dry, disciplined, even humorless and dull. For some of the other executives and managers, the change was disconcerting.

In terms of their annual budget requests, for example, they discovered that the ground rules had completely changed. In the past, they had been expected to present concise, pithy requests that showed the high spots in their projected programs for the coming year. They had been encouraged to look for new ways of doing things in their departments and offices. Innovative programs had been rewarded.

But under Frank Daw, the managers found, what was expected was a detailed, thorough accounting for past performance, and a logical projection of the future. Their experiments and proposed innovations were dismissed as trivial. "There is only one way," Frank often said, "to run an insurance company." And woe to the manager who made an arithmetical error in his or her line-item budget. Frank never missed one.

Frank's other problem was more serious, though he never really understood it. All during his years of steady advancement in the company, he had never spent a day in the field. Frank had no idea what life was like for the salesman or the safety engineer or the claims adjuster. He had never talked to a customer in his life. He had no conception of the unpredictability of the marketplace.

Instead, from his new vantage point, Frank saw a great deal of disorder and lack of method out in the field. People, he was sure, were doing things in a hit-and-miss manner. One of the first things he asked his staff, after he became president, was to prepare a complete manual for the salespeople, one that would "spell out" in detail everything they were supposed to do. He was pleased when a manual in two thick volumes appeared, to be distributed to every salesperson.

When, a few months later, Frank found that sales results hadn't changed, his staff was unable to tell him why. "They must not be following the procedures," he said. When he attended a company-wide meeting of sales managers a little later, and they told him that (a) the sales manual was not only not followed but deliberately ignored, because (b) all the salespeople thought it ridiculous, and furthermore (c) many of the best salespeople were quitting to join other, "less regimented" companies, Frank was surprised and a bit hurt.

At the end of three years as president, precisely on his sixty-fifth birthday, Frank Daw retired. He went home to his lifelong hobbies—raising camellias and collecting stamps. Belatedly, some of the Tradesman's Industrial managers looked with nostalgia at Frank's brief presidency. He had brought a measure of stability and predictability to the company. When he left, Tradesman's Industrial was in its best financial condition in twenty years.

In Frank Daw, we can see that the Analyst approach has its great strengths and its glaring liabilities. The effectiveness of any Style of Thinking is to a great extent a matter of *environment*. That is precisely the point exemplified in Frank Daw's case.

So long as Frank was in his element—accounting, financial statements, data processing—his performance was superb. His talents were just right for the management of such activities. Frank Daw was an exceptionally fine "numbers man." He thrived where that was called for. But he ran into trouble when he had to deal with more ambiguous endeavors—sales, the management and motivation of people, the hectic marketplace—where his attempts to impose "system" and predictability didn't work. As a committed Analyst, he was unable to find a style or an approach that was appropriate for areas where Analyst strategies were simply the wrong ones.

As we have said before, it is not only the Analyst approach that founders when it is inappropriate to the situation. The same is true of any of the Styles of Thinking. If there is a distinction, it may be this: when the Analyst approach goes wrong through inappropriate application, it is so obviously wrong. And that is because of the nature of Analyst strategies. They are so clear-cut, specific, visible, logical. When they are used in the wrong situation, or without skill, we know it at once—though Analysts themselves may not.

On the other hand, when Analyst strategies are used appropriately and they work, one hardly notices. That is because, in the appropriate situation, Analyst strategies are so logical and right.

Chapter VII

THE NO-NONSENSE WAYS OF REALISTS

How to Know a Realist When You See One

Realists tend to have a direct, forceful, frank appearance—not necessarily aggressive, but sometimes that too. They are likely to look you smartly in the eye. They express agreement or disagreement quickly, both verbally and nonverbally. In other words, you usually have a pretty good idea of where you stand with a Realist.

Some favorite Realist expressions are:

"It's obvious to me . . ."

"Everybody knows that . . ."

"Let's look at the facts in the situation . . ."

Realists are quick to express their opinions, and they are more apt than the rest of us to "own" them. That is, they stay away from "weasel words," such as "Don't you think . . . ?" or "Wouldn't you agree that . . . ?" They describe things factually. In order to clarify their meanings they give specific examples, or offer short, pointed, descriptive anecdotes.

Realists are apt to be forthright and positive. At times they may sound dogmatic or domineering, especially if your view of the facts is different from theirs.

Realists enjoy direct, factual discussions of immediate matters, the more practical and down-to-earth the better. They use succinct, pithy, descriptive statements. They dislike talk that seems too theoretical, sentimental, subjective, impractical, or long-winded. They like things short, sweet, and concise. Subtlety is not their strong suit. They can't stand "shaggy dog" stories, but they may like puns and plays on words if they are quickly understandable and have punch. They are often hearty, explosive laughers, and the humor they like best is likely to be down-to-earth if not earthy.

Realist Grand Strategy: Empirical Discovery

Carl Jung talks about four basic functions of the psyche. Of these, the most basic is what is called "Sensing."

> The first point at which the individual meets the outside world is through the senses. He must first establish "the fact that something is there."[1]

What is real in the world is what can be seen, heard, felt, or experienced concretely. The reality of a "fact" is the basic building block of knowledge and understanding for the Realist. Reality cannot be deduced by working from a theory or an abstraction. Reality is *induced* from observation and experience of facts. That is the empirical approach.

When Ignaz Semmelweis in the mid-1800s made the then-startling proposal that it would be a good idea if physicians washed their hands before delivering a baby or performing surgery, he wasn't proceeding from speculation or a theory. He had spent years observing. He had noticed that infections invariably took place when there were unsanitary conditions during surgery, and didn't when a doctor took pains to be clean. Semmelweis' enormously important idea was an empirical discovery.

Most of our knowledge about the world begins with empirical discovery, which leads to a process of trying to make sense of things in a more general way, and eventually to a theory or a concept. The empirical approach is the foundation of much of what we know. It is the Grand Strategy, consciously or unconsciously, of Realists.

[1] Ira Progoff, *Jung's Psychology and Its Social Meaning* (New York: Grove Press, 1953), p. 100.

Realist Strategy #1: Setting Hard Objectives

A group of planners were in a small town in Utah, where the mayor had asked them to do a community survey, in the hope of involving more of the town's citizens in its activities and decisions. Here is a portion of the conversation that went on in one of the group's strategy sessions.

MARTIN (the project leader): I guess there's no doubt that the town is small enough and we have enough people to do a door-to-door survey.

STEVE: Sure. We can get a map and just divide it up between us.

MARK: When should we do it? Saturday, when most people will be at home?

MARTIN: Why not? What's the weather report?

JANE: Martin, what do you suggest as an approach?

MARTIN: Well, what Steve said makes sense to me. Just divide up the map between us and go door to door.

JERRY: But what is it we're going to ask?

MARTIN: Pardon?

JERRY: What exactly are we asking people? I mean, here we are going door to door, talking to them. Shouldn't we all be asking the same questions? And if so, what are they?

JANE: Oh. Good point, Jerry.

JERRY: And do we carry clipboards and take notes, or what?

MARTIN: I think that should be all right.

MARK: Jerry's question raises another point. We're going to have a mountain of notes. How will we deal with that?

MARTIN: Jerry, you look agitated.

JERRY: I'm feeling agitated. We need to get this thing under control.

MARTIN: Okay. What do you suggest?

JERRY: First, we need to decide exactly what questions we're going to ask. Second, we need to agree how we're going to handle the data. Third, when are we going to finish? And finally, what are we going to do with all the information once we've got it? I mean, what's it all going to look like?

MARTIN: Well, it sounds as if Jerry has given us an agenda.

Indeed, Jerry the Realist gave this group an agenda and a plan of action, by asking hard, factual, here-and-now questions. Like the Analyst insisting on structure and a plan, the Realist's insistence on defining objectives is an absolute necessity to almost any organizational or group endeavor—unless the endeavor is purely experimental or speculative, and even then a few Realist questions wouldn't hurt. "What's it going to look like?" is a typical Realist inquiry.

Strangely enough, that sort of question is all too seldom asked. We are constantly amazed at the number of groups and projects that take off on their merry way without a real sense of direction, without a clear picture of the result. It is exactly the area of concrete objective-setting that is sorely needed, and calls for the application of Realist strengths.

Realist Strategy #2: The Resource Inventory

Because Realists rely on the facts, on what is real and immediate, they often excel at the identification of resources. In this they resemble Analysts, in their ability and willingness to look at details and constraints. When we try to get anything done, after all, we are constrained by the resources available, a reality that many of us prefer to ignore.

Raymon R. Bruce, a management consultant and a Realist, is one of the inventors of a career planning process that he calls "The Universe Survey." It works something like this:

In planning your career, the first thing you need to do is conduct a thorough survey of your personal universe. It is helpful to think of it in four categories, or "quadrants."

1. Your environment (where you are).
2. Your operations (what you do).
3. Your goals (where you want to go).
4. Your resources.

It is in this fourth quadrant that Bruce encourages a most sweeping and imaginative survey. All of us have far more resources than we realize—our tools, our skills, and our tangibles are the principal ones. But we also have friends, relations, connections, friends of friends, people who could become resources if we only made ourselves known to them, and so forth. The most important part of the Universe Survey is an exhaustive inventory of all those real and potential resources.

The objective, visual, "What does it look like?" approach so often found in Realists is captured in Bruce's instructions for completing the four quadrants of the Universe Survey:

> Think of a roll of movie film showing some real-life activity. Each frame shows a different picture because things keep changing. You could identify all the important changes very easily by comparing each movie frame with one taken later or another taken previously. . . .[2]

The Universe Survey is a good example of a tool that fits well with Realist skills.

Realist Strategy #3: Getting to Specifics

A group of people in a West Coast hospital were funded for a year by the federal government to undertake a research project in cancer rehabilitation. The group was made up of social workers, psychologists, nurses, a medical doctor, and a psychiatrist. With the exception of the team leader—the psychiatrist, who was an Analyst—the team members proved to be Idealists all.

Their goal, they agreed, was to "find out something" about the differences in treatment between cancer patients who were successfully rehabilitated and those who were not. They set out to interview a large number of patients. The interviewers compiled an enormous amount of information in notes and tape recordings, all of which was transcribed into numerous volumes of typescript. While the interviewers interviewed, the team leader maintained meticulous charts on the number of patients involved, the various

[2] From Raymon R. Bruce and Preston McCoy, "An Approach to Career Development Using the Universe Survey," Copyright 1974 by Universe Survey, Inc., San Francisco.

types of cancer included, medical and psychosocial histories, demographic data, and the like.

The project went on, with apparent smoothness, for nine months. Then it was time for the second-year funding application, which meant, first, a visit by a representative of the funding agency. The visit proved to be a disaster for the project team.

The agency representative spent two or three days looking over the work that the team had done, and then called a meeting. She said something like this:

> "I can see that you have done a great deal of work. You have a staggering amount of data, your records are beautifully kept, and I have no doubt that you've learned a lot. But what? It's impossible to tell where you're going, what results you expect, or what specifically you hope to accomplish. Without some specifics, there is simply no way you'll get funded again."

To which the team leader responded: "Well, you know, this is all a carefully managed exploratory study."

His protest carried no weight, and second-year funding proved to be unobtainable. The group had gone too far and too long without getting to specifics. There were no Realists among its members.

A Realist would have asked the necessary questions long ago, if not at the start of the project. At very least, a Realist would have come up with some useful categories that the group could have used to focus their interviews, sort their data, develop research hypotheses. Realists tend to be good at making categories. So are Analysts. The difference is that Realists determine the categories *after* they've seen how the data falls. Analysts think up categories beforehand based upon what the theory says the data will look like.

Realist Strategy #4: Simplification

"Reduction" is the technical word for this strategy. It is the attempt to reduce a problem to its simplest form. We hear it all the time in discussions of political or social issues.

"It's a simple case of black versus white."

"The problem is the government is growing too large."

"It's simply a matter of educating the public."

"Property taxes have got out of hand, that's the whole problem."

When you hear statements like these, you are hearing the process of Reduction or Simplification, and you are probably hearing a Realist talking. The problem is to decide when the strategy is useful and when it is inappropriate.

In our own firm—four of us—we have learned something about the productive use of the strategy. Three of us love nothing more than to speculate and conceptualize, theorize and hypothesize, analyze and fantasize. We can always tell when the time has come to get down to business—when our fourth member, Susan, begins to look impatient and then says something like, "Look, what the problem really is, is this. . . ." She is more often right than not. Whether right or wrong, her strategy is a useful one because it obliges us to focus our attention on the work at hand. It is a way of "keeping us honest."

Realist Strategy #5: Using Expert Opinion

Realists rely on their senses, on observation and personal experience in a very concrete way, to make sense of things. They rely on objective facts as much as possible in order to solve problems and make decisions. But what if the facts are not clear? What if the problem is obscure, or the decision to be made involves factors that are outside the experience of the Realist?

In such circumstances Realists have little hesitation about relying on expert opinion. "If we don't understand the problem, then let's find someone who does."

Realists indeed rely on expert opinion more than people with other Styles of Thinking. Perhaps they are simply quicker to acknowledge their limitations than others. We think it more likely to be behavior that flows from one of the Realist's strongest needs —the need to have *control* over the situation.

The Realist's thinking process (conscious or not) goes something like this:

So long as the facts are at hand, and so long as I understand them, I am in control of things. Once there are no clear facts, or I don't understand what I'm seeing, I'm in danger of losing control. Therefore, I had better call on someone who can tell me what the facts are.

Not knowing something is itself an immediate fact to the Realist, much more quickly and obviously so than it may be to other people.

The Expert Opinion strategy can be most useful and efficient. The problem, of course, is to know how to find out who is truly an "expert." Or, in other words, if you can't define the problem yourself and you don't know what questions to ask, how do you know the right answers when you hear them? It is a perplexity, which may explain why Realists are more quick both to hire and fire outside experts.

Realist Strategy #6: Incisive Correction

"They cut your hair all wrong. Now you march right back down to the barbershop and tell them to do it properly!"

While we find no significant differences between men and women relative to I_nQ scores, we believe that there is a lot of Realist in a lot of mothers, especially when children are at a certain age. And in nurses—in fact our data show that to be so.

Consider the mother, with a houseful of children, and the nurse, with a ward full of patients. It is all very well to have rules and ideals about how children and patients ought to behave, but daily living is a process of fixing and correcting here, there, and everywhere, all the time. One proceeds empirically. A patient's buzzer sounds, or a child screams with anger or pain, and you respond. You fix the problem if you can. You correct it, and you try to do it in such a way that it stays put for a while.

The corrective quality of the Realist is a very strong one. So is a kind of incisiveness, as we have said before. The two together become a strategy which, used appropriately, can be a most powerful one.

A Realist marriage counselor would sound like this. The client, a housewife, says:

"I don't know what to do. He doesn't pay any attention to me anymore. We never talk. He sits in front of the TV all evening, and goes off to bed without saying good-night. In the morning, he just reads the paper and goes off to work without a word. I don't know what his problem is, but he acts as though I don't exist. Life is just plain dull."

The counselor asks, "Have you ever tried to tell him these things?"

"Oh, of course. But it's like everything else. He won't listen. He doesn't pay attention."

"What would you like to do about it?"

"Well, if things don't get better, I'd just like to leave. Walk out."

"Why don't you tell him that?"

"What?"

"Go home and tell him you're going to leave if he doesn't shape up. Your job is to get his attention. What he does after that is his problem."

Read the columns of "Dear Abby" or Ann Landers in the newspaper. Study their responses to people's problems. Abby and Ann give advice, often spiced with biting humor that is invariably direct, incisive, no-nonsense.

A common difficulty for Realists occurs when they discover that most people don't really want advice, even when they ask for it. What people really want is sympathy, or for others to say nice things and make them feel good. A great many people have a peculiar tendency suddenly to not hear when someone says something direct and incisive to them.

"Here's what I would do if I were you," the Realist says.

Whereupon the response: "That isn't the advice I was looking for."

Incisive Correction, like other sharp tools, is a strategy to be used carefully and judiciously.

Realist Strengths and Liabilities

Not long ago, we were making a presentation on the I_nQ to a convention of state budget and fiscal officers—eighty-five people gathered in a hotel in Sun Valley, Idaho. Everyone had taken the questionnaire, and we had gone through a brief description of the Styles of Thinking. In half an hour we had touched on many of the high points, much as in Chapter II of this book. Then we paused, and asked for questions and comments from the audience.

As usual, questions came thick and fast from all over the room, but our attention was drawn to a silent man, who sat about eight rows back on the center aisle. He was a solidly built fellow, with what could only be described as a determined, intent expression. We noticed that ever since we had described the Realist Style of Thinking, this man had been staring at us, firmly, stonily, almost angrily. Obviously, something was on his mind.

As the questions and answers continued, the intensity of the man's stare increased, he began to look agitated, and at last he could contain himself no longer. In a loud voice he blurted out: "How can you say that Realists believe everybody should agree on the facts? It's perfectly obvious to any sensible person that people *don't* agree most of the time."

All we could do by way of response was to nod and say, "Yes. You're right." The man's demeanor, his growing agitation, his air of being confronted by a dissonant idea and of trying to sort out the facts before he spoke, all were characteristic of a Realist. Even his phraseology—"It's perfectly obvious to any sensible person"— was a typically Realist formulation.

Abstract paintings tend to give Realists trouble. It is important for them to be able to name things. A painting is a fact. But a fact without a name, without a specific identity, causes discomfort for Realists. Like Analysts, they have a relatively low tolerance for ambiguity, and for that reason they are not at their best in un-structured situations, where the data or meaning are not clear.

A woman we know, Mary Ann, makes her living as a teacher in adult education. One of her specialties is courses for Women in Management. Mary Ann holds seminars and works with groups of women in organizations, helping them to define their career opportunities and to formulate action plans for their personal development.

Mary Ann's strength is not in theorizing, or inspiring, or in building detailed plans. Her strength is in getting her clients to ask themselves very specific, "hard" questions:

"Where exactly do I want to be a year or two from now?"
"What are my resources for getting there?"

"What specifically do I have to do in order to meet my objectives?"

"How will I know when I've made it?"

Mary Ann is known, fondly, to some of her clients as a "bulldog." A few of them find her a trifle pushy, and shy away because they don't like to be pushed—which often means having to get specific and to take responsibility. But most of them find Mary Ann's technique helpful. Once they learn to really "face the facts," they find practical ways to achieve their goals.

Because Realists are people of strong opinions, based on perceived facts, they are quick to form opinions of other people. Like all of us, they respect people much like themselves. If you don't stand up to the Realist, he or she is likely not to respect you. You have become a certain kind of "fact" for the Realist. And once having decided on the nature of the facts, it is hard to get Realists to change their minds. That is probably the greatest liability of the Realist Style of Thinking. They come across to others at times like stubborn, unimaginative blockheads.

The thing to remember, both for your dealing with the Realist, and for the Realist dealing with you, is this: "What you see is what you get."

Chapter VIII

COMPATIBILITIES, AFFINITIES, AND
CONFLICTS—HOW THE STYLES
WORK TOGETHER

An Introductory Note

What we have portrayed in the five preceding chapters are what sociologists call "Ideal Types." That is, we have been describing Synthesists, Idealists, Pragmatists, Analysts, and Realists as if, for example, an individual could actually be *all* Analyst in real life.

One of the dangers in any human typology is that its convenience and predictive value lead us to forget that real people are seldom "Ideal Types." Even when the label accurately describes some of their behavior it does not describe all of it. Our troublesome tendency, once we have put labels on people, is to act as if each person so labeled were identical, not at all what these labels ought to mean. They mean only that all of those whom we call Realists or Idealists have something in common although they may be very different in everything else. Most people agree that both hams and pretzels are "salty," yet no one claims they taste the same.

To the extent that our Style of Thinking categories reflect human reality, they should be treated as helpful and useful tools, as aids to a better understanding of ourselves and others. Even if they seem real in isolation, we need to remember that each of us contains and uses different proportions of all five Styles of Thinking at all times.

"Salt and Pepper"

In the rest of this chapter we will look at each of the ten possible two-pronged Style of Thinking combinations. We will also talk in general terms about three-pronged combinations and about the flat I_nQ profile. But we need to set the stage first, with some basic notions about Style of Thinking combinations.

A useful analogy is that of salt and pepper. Every cook (and every eater) knows that salt and pepper have very different qualities, and that there is no such thing as a true "blend" of the two condiments. Both enhance the flavor and the enjoyment of a dish, but they do so in different ways. If we want our food to have more zip, we will add pepper to taste. If we want to increase the flavor of a basic food, and make it less bland, we add salt. It is a matter of taste and preference.

We know that too much salt or too much pepper will destroy the food. Too much of either can be unhealthy, and that also varies between people. But most importantly, salt and pepper are never a true blend. They work separately, even when they are in combination; though some would say there is a kind of third flavor that results when both salt and pepper are combined judiciously. An overall richness is produced, which wouldn't be there without both condiments. That, we suggest, is a useful way to think about the richness of Style of Thinking combinations.

Now, let us look at each of the possible two-pronged combinations. We shall do so in the order of their frequency, as we have come across them so far.

The Idealist-Analyst (IA)

Characteristic of the IA combination is a broad, comprehensive view. The person with the IA orientation wants to achieve the ideal goal using the best method available. The IA is apt to be a planner, in the broad sense, and is unlikely to make quick decisions. Idealist-Analysts frequently come across to others as careful, thoughtful people.

A young man, Rich, recently graduated from high school. He had a distinguished record in science, and received handsome scholarship offers from four prestigious universities.

When it came time to decide which offer to accept, Rich compared the four situations in some very objective ways: the relative value of the stipends, a comparison of travel and living expenses, the quality of each physical facility in terms of the research Rich wanted to do. But he also visited each school in order to evaluate some other factors: the "feel" of the campus, the friendliness and receptivity of the faculty, the kinds of people who would be his fellow students, the community in which each university was situated—the total environment, in other words.

Rich's final choice was founded on both technical and subjective criteria. His approach to the decision was careful and analytical, but it was also open, receptive, and idealistic.

Characteristic of the Idealist-Analyst combination, then, is a broad, future-oriented, planned view of things. IA plans include data about human needs as well as factual, objective data about things like costs and constraints. An individual with this orientation wants to achieve high aims using the best method possible. For instance, we have found the IA combination more frequently among design engineers than in the overall population. We find this reassuring, as we would prefer to cross a bridge designed by someone to whom high standards of quality and accuracy are important.

IAs are unlikely to make quick decisions or snap judgments. Their receptivity to a multitude of possibilities, their commitment to high standards, as well as their desire for data, structure, and predictability, result in considerable time for mulling things over. IAs can be a frustration to people with a quicker, less methodical approach. They can seem to take forever to make a move.

The Analyst-Realist (AR)

The AR combination is characteristic of people who are highly task-oriented and objective, who consider themselves factual, and like structured approaches to problems. The AR combination is one that seeks order, predictability, and control over the situation. The Analyst-Realist is interested in achieving concrete results, and in finding the best method for achieving them.

Margaret is a successful free-lance writer, who excels at investigative reporting. She analyzes the situation which she wants to cover, looks for all the details and fine points, and digs hard and persistently for the facts. When she writes her articles they are fully documented, accurate, and highly readable, written in a clear, concise style and full of specific, down-to-earth examples.

Margaret usually works on one project at a time, seeing it through from beginning to end without distraction. She sticks with it until she sees her words in print, and needless to say she is also a thorough, careful, and meticulous proofreader of her own material.

Analyst-Realists plan things carefully and meticulously, and remain firmly focused on the task to be done. They seldom deviate once the plan is set, and they stick with it until a concrete result has been achieved. That intense focus often generates an extraordinarily forceful quality, which, if well moderated, produces great accomplishments.

The problem that others have with Analyst-Realists is that they sometimes seem too task-oriented. They can become so intent on the job at hand that they seem tunnel-visioned, with no room and no patience for what seems to them trivial or beside the point.

The major shortcoming of the AR combination is a low tolerance for situations that defy either analysis or action. The Analyst component seeks structure and predictability. The Realist mode requires control, action, and concrete results. Confronted by situations where none of these things is possible, Analyst-Realists are at a loss, and usually experience stress. Under such stress, and particularly when under pressure to produce, they are likely either to freeze or to strike out wildly, the favored AR defensive strategies.

Sometimes Analyst-Realists find themselves locked into a totally inappropriate course of action. Needless to say, it is embarrassing when they have to be bailed out by an "irrational" Synthesist or an "expedient" Pragmatist.

The Synthesist-Idealist (SI)

An individual with the SI combination is likely to approach problems in the opposite way from the Analyst-Realist. The SI's focus is on ideals, values, and inferences rather than on plans, structure, and facts. The SI is speculative, process-oriented, and interested in the "Whys" of things (while the AR is interested in the "Whats," the IA in the "Hows").

Synthesist-Idealists report that there are internal conflicts in the combination. The major conflict arises from a contradiction between basic assumptions of the two Styles of Thinking. The Idealist is committed to agreement among people and ideas in the best, most "idealistic," comprehensive way. The Synthesist is constantly aware that such agreement is unlikely or impossible, and that if it occurs at all it is the result of synthesis, the outcome of conflict.

At the level of motivation, the Synthesist wants to be admired, the Idealist is concerned with the needs of others. In the same person, those motivations can bring about real problems of internal stress.

A Synthesist-Idealist reports on a recent experience:

I was working as an administrative adviser in a Middle Eastern country. My clients were a large group of Arab administrators. But I had other clients, too—a small group of American advisers who were actually in charge of the way most things got done in the government.

Quite early in my tour, I discovered that my Arab clients were intuitive, clever, even playful people, charming and open, but generally lacking in our sense of Western "system." The Americans, on the other hand, were quite the opposite— analytical, structured, intent on imposing system everywhere. The two groups seemed quite incompatible.

My assignment was to conduct a number of seminars for the Arab administrators, in order to introduce them to Western management techniques. It was a dilemma for me. I didn't want to impose analytical techniques on intuitive people, yet that was what they wanted to learn, and it was also what I thought was needed in the government.

But the more painful dilemma was in terms of the organization. I saw my Arab and American clients as such opposites. One part of me wanted to find a way to bring them together under some kind of conceptual umbrella. The other part of me wanted to set things up so they would just have at it and somehow come to a resolution. And of course I couldn't choose sides. I was never able to fully resolve my ambivalence, but found myself wavering back and forth between the two approaches throughout the several months I was over there.

In this account, we can see the internal conflict of the Synthesist-Idealist. We can also see another characteristic of the combination. An SI is likely to be seen as someone who is in touch with the broad meaning of things. SIs are interested in the "Whys" of things. The trouble is, they sometimes get so preoccupied with "Why" questions that they never get to the "Whats" or "Hows." Thus Synthesist-Idealists are often seen by others as conceptualizers and theorizers, and not necessarily very practical people.

The Idealist-Realist (IR)

This combination is characterized by a twin thrust of high standards and "concreteness." The IR knows how things "should" be, and has at hand practical steps for reaching the "should." A person with the IR combination may often be seen by others as both receptive and immediately helpful. The IR is likely to show considerable drive toward getting things done and achieving high quality results at the same time.

Nurses often tend to show high preferences for both Idealist and Realist strategies. Consider especially the nature of hospital nursing. Think about the motivations that a person must have if he or she is going to be an effective nurse, one who is satisfied with the job.

Nursing requires a commitment to community and personal service, to supportiveness and helpfulness. This is the Idealist part of nursing. Idealists get their rewards from being helpful, and from the internal satisfactions of the work itself and what they see as its high value. Idealists are often content to be unsung heroes.

The Realist part of the combination in nurses is focused on the practical, concrete, and immediate aspects of the work. There are specific individuals to be cared for, immediate needs to be met. Every act of hospital nursing achieves a concrete result. There is a dressing to be changed, a shot to be administered, a body to be bathed, a patient to be made more comfortable. There is nothing obscure or ambiguous about the act of nursing, and that appeals strongly to the Realist.

Because of such characteristics, Idealist-Realists (not just IR nurses) find themselves overcommitted sometimes, especially to the needs and wants of others. They tend to take on the burdens of others and not to pay enough attention to themselves. And if those they help don't acknowledge the service, IRs feel resentful and ill-used.

The Pragmatist-Realist (PR)

Like the Analyst-Realist, the person with the PR combination is highly task-oriented, but approaches problems in a less structured and deliberate way. The PR is interested in achieving concrete results, but will do so in an experimental, incremental manner. The PR is apt to be someone with considerable energy and drive, who may show a strong need to achieve for the sake of achievement.

> Tom is a young garage owner. What characterizes him more than anything is his high level of energy and drive, his need for doing and achieving. He approaches problems forcefully, but with a willingness to live within limits of available time and money. "How do we get something done, given the present situation?" is the question that comes most often to him, in the often hectic and variable environment of a busy service garage.
>
> Tom is not given to deep thinking, detailed analysis, or long-range planning. Work is a very immediate matter. He makes up his mind quickly about what needs to be done to service a customer's car. Seldom unsure of himself, Tom inspires confidence. However, so confident is Tom of his ability to get things done quickly and surely, sometimes he overextends himself, takes on too much work, and then customers complain over delays that arise from an unforeseen backlog in the garage.

Pragmatist-Realists, then, are prone to make quick decisions, with a minimum of data, and to be more interested in movement and action than in careful planning. When they overuse their preferred approach, PRs can seem impulsive, too quick to move, and are apt to be overextended.

The Idealist-Pragmatist (IP)

The Idealist-Pragmatist will approach problems in a situational, "pragmatic" way, so long as goals are kept in mind and high standards are maintained. The IP combination is typical of a person who gains agreement on goals and then tolerates a great deal of latitude in method. Idealist-Pragmatists are apt to have a high concern for "people issues," and to be tuned in to people's needs.

Harold, a high school teacher, is committed to two basic ideas in his teaching. One is the overall superiority and desirability of active student participation in the classroom. The other is a conviction that each student should be treated as a unique individual, and therefore the approach to teaching should be flexible and should vary with the student.

Harold tries to stimulate participation in his classes, by encouraging open discussion and even selection of topics by the class. He does very little lecturing, and then only when it seems helpful to the class or his opinion is requested. He takes great pains not to impose his own authority or opinions on the students.

At the same time, Harold actively practices the principle of "It all depends." When a student expresses a strong, dogmatic opinion about something, Harold gently urges the person to look at other possible viewpoints. When he is asked for his opinion on some point, he offers three or four choices, and suggests that it depends on the situation. No opinion or theory presented by a student is ever completely wrong or completely right in Harold's view.

To some of his students, Harold's teaching style seems admirable. They appreciate the freedom they have, the latitude that Harold allows them. They enjoy the informality, the absence of structure. But other students condemn Harold for exactly the same things. They say that he doesn't "deliver" enough, that the students are left to flounder. They want more direction and more structure from him.

The Idealist-Pragmatist leadership style is apt to appear overly permissive to many people, because it combines receptivity with adaptability. It is uncomfortable for people, such as Analyst-Realists, who value structure and order. The IP approach can seem to them quite lacking in limits and constraints, without predictability. It appears to them a style of "non-leadership."

The Analyst-Pragmatist (AP)

"Controlled experiment" is the key notion for describing the AP approach. The Analyst-Pragmatist is a person who values structure and predictability, knows where he or she is going and generally how to get there, but is willing to experiment along the way. A kind of structured playfulness is likely to characterize the thought processes of the Analyst-Pragmatist: "Let's see, here's where I want to go. Here's how to get there. Now what might be fun and profitable to do along the way?"

Pamela is a young woman of twenty-two who has established her own business as a free-lance legal secretary. When she left high school, Pamela was not interested in going on to college. She preferred the idea of being independent, of moving directly into the adult world. She also wanted to be financially independent. The problem was how to do that with only a high school diploma.

The most likely route, she thought, was to become a secretary. She knew she was bright and had good verbal skills. On the other hand, most secretaries didn't make very good money, she knew.

So Pamela carefully analyzed the situation, and discovered that she could make more money if she became a legal secretary. She signed up for a course in a business school, and because of her quickness and learning ability, she soon mastered the necessary skills.

Pamela spent a year, on her first job, learning basic office routines. As she worked, she found that she could have even more value in the marketplace if she picked up some office management skills. So when work was light, she persuaded her employer to let her look over such things as files and court schedules in order to learn about them and recommend improvements. And along the way, she picked up some experience in legal research.

After three years of reasonably well-paid apprenticeship, Pamela decided to go it on her own. With her former employers as willing, if not happy, references, she prepared a brochure and mailed it to all the smaller law offices in her area. Now she has more work offered to her than she can handle. She is selective, working when and where she wants to.

Pamela's success is due to a shrewd and deliberate application of her natural Analyst and Pragmatist strategies. She set a clear plan for herself, performed careful analyses when needed, and was willing to experiment and adapt along the way to get where she wanted to go.

The major liability of the Analyst-Pragmatist is a tendency to approach all life situations in a manner which often appears to others as calculating and manipulative. That perception can be especially damaging in interpersonal relations. The AP seems to have a grand design in mind, and can seem tactically opportunistic in trying to fulfill it.

The Analyst-Synthesist (AS)

This combination is characterized by a respect for structure and logic, together with an understanding and valuing of the opposite. The AS can be a planner who also takes the trouble to develop a counterplan. The combined interest in speculation and theoretical method may seem, to others, out of touch at times with the real, concrete world. But other things being equal, the combination can have immense intellectual and conceptual power.

Larry is a systems analyst for a chain of hospitals in California. His job is to design health service delivery methods for an organization made up of half a dozen hospitals, several thousand physicians, and up to a million potential patients.

Larry relishes the challenge, the scope of his job. He loves to draw grandiose, complicated designs. In his office he has two huge blackboards, each of which covers an entire wall. On one he has sketched in great detail a model of the whole hospital system as it exists today. On the other he has spread an equally complicated but elegant design of a system that would work just as well, but that is based on completely opposite premises from the first.

Larry is known in his organization as a conceptualizer. He has a combined interest in speculation and logic. He tries to conceptualize his designs in a way that is both as broad and abstract as possible and as detailed as possible. Thus he can talk both theory and everyday reality—people are impressed with his intellectual scope.

Systems theorist C. West Churchman suggests that for every plan, no matter how logical and reasonable, there is a counterplan that is just as good. Analyst-Synthesists are more aware of that than anyone. That is a source of great excitement for them. It is also the potential source of an extreme sort of internal conflict. A basic Analyst assumption is that the world is (or should be) logical, rational, and orderly. A basic Synthesist assumption is quite the opposite of that. The conflict for the Synthesist-Analyst is between an awareness of logic and absurdity, of order and conflict, of "system" and the absence of it. Such polar contradictions can cause internal stress, and can lead to behavior that is most confusing to others.

Synthesists tend to believe that they have important, even profound things to say. They need to believe that people are listening. Analysts tend to believe that they have logical, thought-out things to say, which people should also be patient enough to listen to. Put together, the two sets of tendencies can be formidable if, at times, exhausting.

The Synthesist-Pragmatist (SP)

The SP combines the speculative with the adaptive, the dialectic with the eclectic, the conflict-oriented approach with the contingency approach, an interest in change with an interest in innovation. In other words, we believe that the SP shows the highest tolerance for ambiguity and uncertainty of any I_nQ orientation. Synthesist-Pragmatists should be able to live comfortably in a changing, uncertain world better than the rest of us.

With the SP, we have an image of someone on a high wire, constantly suspended in space, and loving every minute of it; perhaps fearful because of the absolute unpredictability of things, yet utterly stimulated and fascinated by it at the same time.

The Synthesist-Pragmatist is apt to be an individual who is short on patience with prolonged analysis, excessive sentimentality, or formalistic methods. As a leader, the SP is likely to be seen as someone who likes to keep things stirred up, with little regard for stability, endurance, or the status quo. SPs are also likely to be people who are perceived as having considerable creative energy, though given their giddy, relatively lonely vantage point they may keep that part of themselves under wraps, for fear of scaring off all those who value structure and predictability.

The Synthesist-Realist (SR)

Here is the rarest of all I_nQ combinations, in terms of the data we have gathered in three years of research. The Synthesist and the Realist are at opposite ends of the thinking spectrum. Synthesist and Realist assumptions are opposed and conflicting in most respects, as are their strategies, techniques, and values. It should follow that a person with high preferences in both dimensions would experience a good deal of internal conflict.

The Realist can see and size up the facts of a given situation, objectively and empirically. The drive is there to take action, to move as Realists do. If there is a clear problem, a necessary corrective action is also clear and obviously called for. But then the Synthesist confronts the Realist and says, in effect, "Wait a minute! How do you know those are the facts that you claim you are seeing so clearly? Reality may be quite the opposite. You Realists are easily fooled by appearances."

The way to deal with the conflict is easy to describe, though rather less easy to carry out. What is called for is a deliberate focus on the situation, followed by a confident application of the appropriate strategies. If the situation confronting the Synthesist-

Realist is clear-cut, structured, well-defined, and can be sorted out empirically, then Realist strategies are indicated. If, on the other hand, the situation is ambiguous, unstructured, laden with values and conflict, then one deliberately moves toward the Synthesist approach.

What is required is a pause, a skipped beat, sometimes a brief internal debate, before the proper strategy is chosen. In effect, a decision on strategy has to precede action.

The Synthesist-Realist combination works effectively when the two Styles are properly orchestrated. The potential power of the combination comes from the incisiveness found in each Style of Thinking, and the motivation for movement and achievement common to both Styles. The SR teacher, for example, may be strong on speculation and theory but also deeply interested in their practical applications—a bonus for the student.

When the two Styles are working in a complementary way, the Synthesist-Realist may be a person with great energy for unorthodox but firm achievement. We think of the "creative entrepreneur": a person who, once decided on a direction, moves forcefully, firmly, and imaginatively, but understands that going in the opposite direction would probably have been just as fruitful.

The great potential liability of the SR combination is the possibility of a paralyzing ambivalence. When one sees clearly the proper way to go, and sees just as clearly that the exact opposite is just as attractive, an individual may not move at all; or may strike out impulsively in an entirely new and strange direction just to end the agony.

The "Three-Way" Thinker

Only 2 percent of the people who have taken the I_nQ show this phenomenon—three scores each at a level of sixty or more. If you are a Three-Way Thinker, we suggest that you review the descriptions of all three of your preferred Styles, and think about how they might operate in combination. We have given you enough information by now that you should be able to draw your own conclusions. The difference is that the "salt and pepper" analogy may not work for you. Instead, think of "salt and pepper *and* paprika," or whatever your preferred condiment might be.

The positive aspect of the Three-Way Thinker is that the individual is likely to have more readily available options or strategies with which to work than the One-Way or Two-Way Thinker. In other words, he or she may be more versatile, able to respond differently to varying situations. The important thing may be the relative balance of those preferences across the I_nQ spectrum.

What might be of most benefit to you in terms of your personal development is to focus on your two least-preferred Styles of Thinking. This can tell you something about your blind spots, and can help you to identify the strategies and approaches that are relatively underutilized. They might profitably be worked on toward being an even more well-rounded thinker.

The "Flat" Profile

The person with a flat I_nQ profile is likely to be less predictable, less intense, and probably less recognizable than people with strong stylistic preferences. He or she may have more options, and be more "adaptable" in the broad sense. The problem is that the behavior arising out of strong stylistic preferences often lends a kind of identity or recognition by others to a person, which may not be as clear for the person with a flat profile.

On first glance, one might assume that the person with a flat profile is little different from a Pragmatist. But there is an important difference. Depending on the strength of his or her preference, the Pragmatist uses the incremental, contingent, "whatever works" approach as a purposeful, conscious strategy more often than not, while the person with a flat profile uses any set of strategies either situationally or more or less at random.

The problem, if there is one, occurs at the behavioral level. There is evidence that charisma is associated with strong I_nQ preferences. Our experience confirms the notion. People with high personal impact, who are more or less predictable, and who stand out in a group (either positively or negatively) tend consistently to have strong Style of Thinking preferences. The image of the individual with a flat profile may be one of a "nice" person who gets along with everyone, and who goes along with the flow of events. Whether or not that is seen as a problem or a liability by the individual depends on what one values.

"Well, That's All Very Interesting, But . . ."

We have given you a description of all the Styles of Thinking and their combinations. We have talked about the strategies favored by the different Styles, a few clues for recognizing and understanding them have been offered, and you have some idea of the strengths and liabilities of each.

To the extent that our Style of Thinking scheme seems real to you, you understand more than you did previously about how you operate—how you approach situations, ask questions, make decisions, and solve problems. You may also have had some insights about certain other people—especially, we hope, those whom you find hard to understand and who give you trouble in one way or another.

But you may be thinking something like this:

> "Well, that's all very interesting. I certainly find your ideas intriguing. It's nice to know about and all that. But now that I know I'm an Idealist or a Realist or whatever, so what? What do I do with it? What's it all good for?"

The crucial question is, Do these ideas have practical value? What that usually means is, Will understanding these ideas change my life in any way? Can I use them to become a more effective manager, leader, follower, or just plain man or woman? If so, how?

You now have a better understanding of the profound influence that a person's thinking style has on his or her effectiveness and comfort. You know a good deal about how different Styles of Thinking determine behavior. You can use that knowledge to do these things:

—Learn to influence other people more effectively, in order to get done what you want to get done; to help achieve your own goals.
—Increase the thinking strengths that you already possess, to make them more powerful and efficient.

—Learn new techniques and strategies, to become more versatile decision makers and problem solvers.

—Learn to be better at avoiding errors in perception and judgment.

In the following chapters we will suggest ways for accomplishing these things.

Chapter IX

INFLUENCING OTHERS

What "Influencing" Means

How do you go about influencing other people?

We can imagine some of the responses:

"Why, I just try to be myself, that's all."

"I say what I have to say. I do what needs to be done. What else?"

"Well, I try to meet people halfway, if possible. That seems only sensible."

"I do whatever works, depending on the situation."

"Whatever do you mean? I don't try to influence people. They either agree with me or they don't."

Each of these responses is based on common sense—depending on your particular view of common sense. What we have to offer by way of strategies and approaches to influencing other people is also based on common sense. The difference in our approach is this: we offer some methods for *focusing* your natural common sense. Methods for influencing are ways to make your influencing efforts more *purposeful, deliberate, and conscious.*

Most of us spend the greater part of our lives trying to influence others, whether consciously or not, whether we like it or not. We try to exert our influence from the moment we emerge from the womb. At first we are seeking food or comfort or love. As we grow we seek safety, belonging, self-esteem. In time we may seek wealth or fame—or merely tranquillity and peace of mind. In all of these quests we are constantly involved in a process of influencing— even when we are trying to influence others just to leave us alone!

There are two basic reasons for improving our skills in influencing people:

First, to make better contact with others, so as to get a better hearing for our own views.

Second, to avoid rubbing people the wrong way, a situation which causes stress for both parties.

Some General Rules

Lawyers, therapists, politicians, salespeople, and poker players— all are conscious of the influencing techniques they use and are usually quite deliberate with them. For many of us, though, our techniques are not as fully recognized as such. They seem simply the way we do things, the "natural" way to act, or "what everyone does." In fact, some people would feel insulted if they were told that they used techniques, whether good or bad, in dealing with others. Knowingly or not, however, the ways we influence others are affected by our Style of Thinking preferences.

Here are the influencing techniques we have seen most commonly used by each Style of Thinking.

Realists approach others in a straightforward, no-nonsense way. "Here are the facts," they say. "This is my opinion." With their strong desire for factual agreement and consensus, Realists are likely to be relatively assertive about seeking those things. "We can all agree about the realities of the situation." One of their most powerful techniques for influencing is based on their incisiveness and immediacy. "Here is what's happening, and here is what we ought to do about it." The Realist's favored technique is to try to mobilize people around objective agreement, in order to move toward concrete corrective action.

Analysts influence others through logic, careful explanation, the use of data that support their arguments. "It is only logical," "It stands to reason," they say. Rather than being aggressive or emotionally persuasive, Analysts assume that others are—or should be —swayed by the convincing logic and rationality of what they have to say. They present themselves as eminently sensible, reasonable people, and have expectations that others will be more or less the same.

Pragmatists exert influence simply by being enthusiastic and eager. They will try to motivate others with their relative quickness and playfulness. "Say, I'll buy that." "What do you think of this bright idea?" Being adaptable and given to tactical thinking, Pragmatist influencing behavior is likely to be more flexible than that of other Styles. Pragmatists will look for ways to tap into others' motivations by experimenting with approaches that are likely to work, considering the others' immediate situation. Tom Sawyer's influencing of his friends to paint his aunt's board fence comes to mind as an example.

Idealists influence others by appealing to such things as broad goals and high standards. As we have seen, they are given to a search for aids to agreement: "Don't you think?" "It seems to me." "Can we all agree on this?" They are listeners, and head nodders, and they rely on receptivity as a means of bringing people to agreement on the proper view of things.

Synthesists, finally, do less than anyone else to influence others, partly because they understand how hard it is for true agreement to be reached and partly because they accept the "reality" that, in fact, several realities may exist. Synthesists often attempt to overwhelm the other person with their profundity. "May I suggest that we distinguish between . . ." they will say, or "But there's yet another side to the picture." Provided they can find others who are willing to let them, Synthesists will try to influence through debate, pointed argument, or the kind of structured exchange of wit —leaping back and forth between logic and absurdity—as befits their dialectical approach.

What follows from these thumbnail accounts is this: Our influencing techniques are styled largely for gaining agreement with, and rewards from, people who are much like ourselves. We base our understanding of others and their motivations on what we think we know of ourselves and our motivations. We then decide that our way is both the "right" way and the "normal" way. All of us, to one extent or another, tend to fall into the trap of assuming that "everyone is like me."

The hard reality is that people really are different. We discover, sometimes to our chagrin or sorrow, that our "right" influencing methods don't necessarily work on others. "They won't listen to reason," "He certainly looks at things in an odd way," are phrases

BEHAVIORAL CLUES

What to look and listen for	Synthesist	Idealist
Apt to appear:	Challenging, skeptical, amused; or may appear tuned out, but alert when disagrees.	Attentive, receptive; often supportive smile, head nodding, much verbal feedback.
Apt to say:	"On the other hand . . ."	"It seems to me . . ."
	"No, that's not necessarily so . . ."	"Don't you think that . . . ?"
Apt to express:	Concepts, opposite points of view; speculates, may identify absurdities.	Feelings, ideas about values, what's good for people, concerns about goals.
Tone:	Sardonic, probing, skeptical; may sound argumentative.	Inquiring, hopeful; may sound tentative or disappointed and resentful.
Enjoys:	Speculative, philosophical, intellectual argument.	Feeling-level discussions about people and their problems.
Apt to use:	Parenthetical expressions, qualifying adjectives and phrases.	Indirect questions, aids to gain agreement.
Dislikes:	Talk that seems simplistic, superficially polite, fact-centered, repetitive, "mundane."	Talk that seems too data-bound, factual, "dehumanizing"; and openly conflictual argument unless about issues of caring or integrity.
Under stress:	Pokes fun.	Looks hurt.
Stereotype:	"Troublemaker"	"Bleeding Heart"

TO STYLES OF THINKING

Pragmatist	Analyst	Realist
Open, sociable; often a good deal of humor, interplay, quick to agree.	Cool, studious, often hard to read; may be a lack of feedback, as if hearing you out.	Direct, forceful; agreement and disagreement often quickly expressed nonverbally.
"I'll buy that . . ."	"It stands to reason . . ."	"It's obvious to me . . ."
"That's sure one way to go . . ."	"If you look at it logically . . ."	"Everybody knows that . . ."
Non-complex ideas; may tell brief personal anecdotes to explain ideas.	General rules; describes things systematically, offers substantiating data.	Opinions; describes factually, may offer short, pointed anecdotes.
Enthusiastic, agreeable; may sound insincere.	Dry, disciplined, careful; may sound set, stubborn.	Forthright, positive; may sound dogmatic or domineering.
Brainstorming around tactical issues; lively give-and-take.	Structured, rational examination of substantive issues.	Short, direct, factual discussions of immediate matters.
Case examples, illustrations, popular opinions.	Long, discursive, well-formulated sentences.	Direct, pithy, descriptive statements.
Talk that seems dry, dull, humorless; or too conceptual, philosophical, analytical, "nit-picking."	Talk that seems irrational, aimless, or too speculative, "far-out"; and irrelevant humor.	Talk that seems too theoretical, sentimental, subjective, impractical, "long-winded."
Looks bored.	Withdraws.	Gets agitated.
"Politician"	"Great Stone Face"	"Blockhead"

that reflect the puzzlement we feel when facts that seem obvious to us have no effect on those we are trying to influence.

Here are two basic rules of thumb:

—The methods and techniques that you customarily use to influence others work best (or work only) with people like yourself—people who share similar values, motivations, and Styles of Thinking. If you want to be effective in influencing people who are different from yourself, you must learn and apply the techniques that are appropriate for them.

—If you want to be truly effective in influencing people who are different from yourself, you must learn something about their motivations, values, and Styles of Thinking. You can do that by observing them and matching their behavior to the descriptions we have given earlier. To make that easier, we have summarized and displayed the descriptions in a chart—"Behavioral Clues to Styles of Thinking."

Now we will look in practical detail at the influencing techniques that work best with each Style of Thinking. Remember that we are describing them as Ideal Types. You will often be influencing people with mixed styles or a combination of styles, so you will have to take a situational approach. Remember the "salt and pepper" analogy and experiment.

Here is a set of preliminary steps for doing that:

1. Look at the specific situation.

2. Look at your respective roles in the situation—yours and that of the person you want to influence.

3. Try out one approach, the one that seems best to fit the other person's Style and the situation.

4. Modify your approach as needed.

5. Think about what happened, as soon after the interaction as possible, and ask yourself what else you might have done.

The influencing techniques will be introduced in a different order this time—the order of frequency with which you are likely to encounter someone with a preference for each Style of Thinking.

GILDING THE GOLDEN RULE—
INFLUENCING IDEALISTS

Remember that Idealists believe in laudable goals, high standards, and good works. Appeal to those high values that they hold. Idealists like to believe that they live by the Golden Rule, and they are firmly convinced that the Golden Rule was written by an Idealist. It probably was.

This does not necessarily mean that Idealists know rightness, goodness, and wholesomeness when they see it. Quite the contrary, in fact. When they overuse their receptivity they can be gullible. If you are actually a wolf in sheep's clothing, you aren't necessarily in trouble with the Idealist, so long as you are good at disguises. The Idealist would much prefer to see the sheep than acknowledge the wolf.

In trying to influence Idealists, don't be overly deceived that their receptivity—their tolerance for alternatives, diverse viewpoints, differing views—means a lack of inner fortitude. The danger is in assuming that because of such preferences, they can easily be influenced or even run over. Not so if they are inwardly convinced of the rightness, the propriety, or the ethics of a certain course of action or a certain code of conduct. Under such circumstances, Idealists can be extremely firm, even rigid. Their disappointment in you may show through as almost parental scolding. Often, however, their dissatisfactions may be concealed. They may keep their faith inwardly, and seem to agree with everything you say or suggest, just to keep from having to hurt your feelings or avoid a distressing confrontation. If they must confront you they will try to do it in a way that is so gentle it may verge on indirectness.

With these cautions in mind, let us proceed to a number of specific techniques that work well with Idealists.

"Can You Help Me with My Problem?"

Whenever possible, tap into the Idealist's developmental strength. Idealists like being helpful. They like being seen that way, and they feel rewarded by a chance to assist in the solving of someone else's problem. Their strength is in helping others develop solutions.

Bureaucracies ought to place people with Idealist tendencies in those positions that have primary public contact—the receptionists at the telephone company, the people at the bank information desks, the intake counselors at the welfare agency. Sensitive management wants to have people out there who will be receptive to clients and customers and will soften the blow of first contact with the organization. Who better than Idealists?

Here's how *not* to approach that Idealist. A determined Realist, let us say, is new in town and has had to wait for a telephone several weeks longer than he or she thinks is appropriate. The Realist strides into the telephone office: "Look! I've been waiting for my #@*+%&(! telephone for six weeks now. When am I going to get some action?!" Understandable, sure. But nothing is surer to throw Idealist receptionists into a tizzy and reduce them to incompetence or hidden resistence. (If that had been the initial approach of our Realist, no wonder it's taking so long to get that phone.)

A better way would have been: "Say, I have a bit of a problem, and I wonder if you could help me with it?" Assuming your Idealist has any power whatsoever to help you, this way is much more likely to enlist that power for you and not against you.

Appeal to High Standards

"Our proposal, Mr. Social Agency Administrator, is based on a broad view of the role of your agency in this city. The new system that we would like you to consider does not merely stress efficiency, though that is one of our criteria. The effectiveness of your information system rests just as much on the satisfaction and motivation of your staff, the agency's relationship with the community, and the overall quality of client services. I think you will see that our plan takes all those things into account."

Here a salesman for a computer software company performs a most effective job of influencing. Perhaps he has spent enough time with the administrator to have a fairly good idea that he has an Idealist viewpoint. But even if not, the approach is likely to be a sound one. The odds are good that anyone connected with running a social agency will have a strong Idealist preference. A situational approach has been taken, making use of the best information available.

If the situation turns out to be different, the salesman's approach can be modified. Meanwhile, covering all the bases and providing a focus on overall goals and high standards are likely to be an effective opening of the influencing process.

"Keep In Touch"

If you are trying to influence an Idealist, to make a sale or get business or recruit him or her into a community cause, keep in mind the likelihood that a quick decision isn't going to be made (especially true if the person is an Idealist-Analyst). A "deal" isn't going to be closed on the first encounter. Idealists need to be helped, supported, and encouraged gently toward a decision. Part of that process involves keeping yourself accessible and in contact. It is a way of demonstrating your own steadfastness and commitment, qualities that Idealists value.

The key phrase here isn't "following up." That is likely to appeal to more objective people. The key is to "keep in touch," which establishes the personal, nonaggressive, relational tone that the Idealist welcomes.

Successful free-lance people, such as photographers, writers, and designers, find the technique not only a good one, but essential. When you are dependent on many clients for your livelihood, sometimes a great deal of time must be spent just reminding them now and then that you are alive and available. But when the clients are Idealists, one should avoid being too pushy, and "selling" every time, or even being too enthusiastic with specific proposals. Just keeping in touch is sufficient.

Help Them Not to Be Nice

Once again: Idealists put great value on supportiveness and receptivity. They don't want to distress others or to hurt their feelings. Hence they can be masters (or mistresses) of overagreement. They will listen, and nod, and say "Uh-huh," and give you encouraging smiles, and make you feel welcome and invite you to "*Please* keep in touch."

You go away thinking you've made a sale, or a contract is in the bag, or this person is going to be the most wonderful contact in the future—and nothing ever happens. You call back and they don't return your calls. Or they're always "out." If you do happen to catch them despite themselves, they say, "Gosh, I really have been thinking about you. But you know how hard it is to get anything done around here." And then: "But it was really good talking to you. Do keep in touch."

With many Idealists, the hardest thing to get them to do is say something negative. If they don't like you, or what you're about, they would rather "receptive" you into exhaustion and oblivion.

You need to read the signals, and then, once you have spotted the cracks in the Idealist's agreeableness, begin to narrow down to the source. Keep probing, gently. Your task is to help the Idealist voice his or her concerns.

"I have the impression you aren't so sure about this part of the proposal." (That's it! Don't force the person, and suspend just the hint of a question mark at the end of your statement.)

"What do you think about this aspect? Some people I've talked to aren't at all sure about it." (Good idea! Don't leave the Idealist standing out there alone. Idealists need support.)

And here is a surefire one: "Now that I think about it, I'm not so sure of this myself. Could you help me clarify it?"

Avoid Conflict Like the Plague!

It is important for two kinds of people to watch themselves carefully, lest Idealists think they are being argued with or are going to wind up in some kind of unpleasantness.

Synthesists must learn to be nice. That is, they must remember that Idealists believe we can all agree just so long as we set our goals high enough, broad enough, or far enough in the future. Equally as important, they must remember that Idealists take things more seriously than Synthesists. Don't take the risk of letting them think you are making fun of them or their ideas. In other words, play down that choice but skeptical witticism.

Realists need to remember that their straightforward, concise, self-assured approach is often nothing but a red flag for the Idealist. Idealists run for cover, or become resentful and resistant, when a strong Realist comes at them. It just isn't *nice* to be so overly aggressive.

THE DOTTED I—INFLUENCING ANALYSTS

The delightful thing about dealing with Analysts is that it is no trouble at all finding ways to influence them. All we have to do is meet them on their own grounds, and approach them in exactly the way they would approach others, as if the world were only populated by sensible, rational people.

But that is easy to say, and much more difficult to do. There are two reasons for that:

First, Analysts are much better at it than the rest of us. They have had all their lives to perfect their skills in order, logic, and being sensible. For the rest of us to be that way is at best a rather clumsy effort compared with what Analysts themselves are capable of.

Second, Analysts are not obtuse, no matter how much others of us may accuse them of it—no more than the rest of us, anyway. Perceptive Analysts have been around long enough to know their own kind when they see them, and to have a sharp eye for pretenders. They have developed their species-specific perceptive skills to a high degree. They know the difference between a genuinely dotted *i* and one that is mere afterthought, for show.

If you want to influence an Analyst, you need to act as an Analyst yourself. You aren't likely to be very good at it the first time around unless you already are one. Therefore you should expect to fail the first few times. Analyst-influencing takes a great deal of practice, but it can be learned.

Learn to Love the Great Stone Face

In any influencing process, the first problem is the initial impression and the very first transaction. It has to do with Transactional Analysis founder Eric Berne's phrase: "What do you say after you say, Hello?"[1] For many of us, that can be a very heavy

[1] From the book of the same name, published in 1972 by Grove Press, New York.

question, and never more so than when we are intent on forming some sort of productive relationship with an Analyst.

The problem is that Analysts aren't much for giving feedback. They aren't lively and twinkling like many Pragmatists, skeptical and sardonically amused like Synthesists, alert and incisive in their responses like Realists. Above all, Analysts aren't receptive and supportive like Idealists. They don't smile and nod and make warm sounds of encouragement. *They just sit there.*

If you're especially fortunate, an Analyst may at least stare at you, or may even nod once or twice, but not in a supportive way, not intentionally as a form of feedback—merely to demonstrate the fact that he or she is still there. A typical Analyst attitude is to sit quietly, perhaps light up (male Analysts are often partial to the structured routine of pipe smoking), and stare off into space or out the window. Meanwhile you sit there trying to influence— selling or negotiating or persuading or whatever, while your enthusiasm, confidence, and cool fade away. The phenomenon is what we call the Analyst Great Stone Face.

For many of us, this kind of transaction can be most disconcerting. It is as if you are talking to a wall or a holograph. Some of us find ourselves blathering nonsensically after a time. There are no clues, there is no feedback to tell you if you are on track or simply making a fool of yourself.

At best, it may seem as if the Analyst is simply hearing you out. And that is exactly what is happening. So the first rule is: Don't be thrown by the lack of feedback. Two possible things can be effective, especially after you've had some practice:

1. Keep your composure, and go ahead with your presentation, pitch, report, or whatever it is. Go through it from A to Z, and be sure it is structured, logical, well-formulated, and thorough. Forget the show biz, the idealism, the dramatic effects. Just do it. Then sit back and wait. Be prepared for a long silence. You will be rewarded at last with a response of some sort. If you manage to out-silence the Analyst, he or she will probably respect you for it.

2. Make your own feedback. At critical points in your presentation, where it is important to know whether or not you're on track, pause, change your tone of voice slightly, and

say, "Does that make sense?" or "Does that seem reasonable to you?" The most you may get is a vaguely affirmative grunt, but count your blessings. What may happen is that the Analyst says, "Go on, go on. Let's hear the whole thing." Then you know you are being listened to.

Behind the Great Stone Face, there is probably an alert, critical mind. Analysts, because of their ability to concentrate, to focus analytically on one thing at a time, are often superb listeners. They just show it differently.

Do Your Homework
Never make a report or a presentation to an Analyst in a slipshod, quick-and-dirty manner. Remember, for them thoroughness and accuracy equate with competence. You must make sure you have done a careful, orderly job of preparation, *especially* the details. Cross all your t's, dot your i's, and above all make sure your numbers are correct.

But no matter how well-prepared you think you are, when you are trying to influence Analysts you should always be prepared for them to find the flaws in your argument. If and when that happens, here are some pointers:

1. Don't get defensive or flustered. Analysts do not care that much how *you* feel about anything. If you think you can chance it, you might even say something like, "Say, it's fortunate you discovered that."
2. If you are wrong or something is missing, own up to it without lengthy explanation. Let them know that you know where to find the answer and when you will do it.
3. Let them have their fun. Especially when you know that you have presented a brilliant, thorough, and well-documented argument, you are likely to see a dry twinkle in the other person's eye when the Analyst performs a successful nit-pick. It's fun for them. Enjoy it with them, though not too boisterously.

Be Logical, Be Orderly
Both of us have had similar experiences in our younger years,

working for Analyst bosses. Each of us has a high Synthesist preference and so we were always full of plans and new ideas.

For much too long, we would take our proposals in to share them with the boss to get his approval or concurrence. We were in the habit of presenting just the high spots, concisely but not always neatly. Often we would enthuse about the benefits of our proposals in glowing, idealistic ways, and sometimes we would stress the originality of our ideas.

But our bosses would just sit there. They would seldom say yes or no. At the most, they might say, "Put it in writing," and then we were lucky if we ever heard of our bright new ideas again.

Then, somehow, we figured it out (independently, as it happened, and both with some outside consultant help). We realized that, earnestly and with enthusiasm, we had been trying to influence our bosses in quite the wrong way. We took steps to correct the situation.

The next time we had a bright idea for a new program, we would write it out in complete detail—factually, objectively, leaving nothing out. We fully outlined what we wanted to do, why it was a good thing to do and why it might not be, what it would cost, how long it would take, and exactly what would happen, step by detailed step. To back up our presentations, we prepared a great chart, which set the whole thing out visually, all in a neat, logical array of boxes and arrows.

Our experiences were fascinatingly similar. In one case, when the appointment time came, the report was handed to the boss and each box and arrow was explained just as carefully and unemotionally as possible. The result was astounding. His face lit up. He smiled and said, "At last you've brought me something I can understand." In the second case, the boss simply broke in during the presentation with "Boy, this looks good. Let me see if my boss is free—he'll want to see this."

It didn't really matter that much of what we wanted to do was actually experimental, to some extent indeterminate and even risky. We had presented the proposal in a way that made the project plans as concrete, orderly, and logical as possible—just like our Analysts.

Let Them Data You to Death

Not only do Analysts require a lot of data from you, in order to be influenced they also need to give a great deal of it back. It is their way of demonstrating their competence, and feeling competent is important to them. They do that by telling you more about the subject than you ever wanted to know.

Let us say that I have gone to call on George, an attorney, in his law office. I am anxious to get his support on a new neighborhood park bond issue that is coming up in the next election. George is an influential fellow in town, and my aim is to get his name on a list of sponsors for a newspaper ad.

Naturally, I have become an "expert" on the subject of neighborhood parks and bond issues. I have done an enormous amount of homework, and I am feeling confident that, if George can be persuaded by the thoroughness of anyone's facts, he has to be by mine.

George hears me out for five minutes. That's about as long as it takes to lay out a fairly detailed explanation of the situation. I sit back, waiting for his questions, confident that I have a thousand more facts to offer in response.

Much to my surprise and chagrin, George then proceeds to regale me with a fifteen-minute lecture on the ins and outs, pros and cons, history and prospects, of my very own bond issue. He knows bonds backward and forward. He knows every detail of the voting process, every fiscal number. He has three times as much data on my subject as I have.

My heart sinks as I listen. But I nod and agree when George makes a good point, I stay silent when I see a flaw in his argument, I swim in his data. When he is through he cheerfully signs the sponsor list. He even compliments me on the thoroughness of my preparation.

There is a variation on this technique. It is called "asking extensional questions." The variation is most useful when, frankly, you are interested in moving an Analyst out of what seems like an untenable position or bringing one over from the opposition.

The method goes like this. When the Analyst makes a statement with which you don't agree, and you believe you have the facts to prove him or her wrong, say: "Exactly what will happen during the year if we put your plan into effect?"

Then sit back. Don't interrupt. What you hope will happen is that your Analyst will discover for himself, or herself, those contradictions or misapplied facts that you have so brilliantly uncovered. You have "flowed with" Analysts' greatest strength—more than others they truly care about data and logic. Extensional questions get Analysts to review their own plans *but* the atmosphere is such that they need not defend their logic or prove to you that their way is the best way. When Analysts are finished with the inevitably detailed exposition, they may have seen the flaws in their own thinking. Well, you knew it all the time—but now they do, too. If you have additional facts, and you present them with well thought out logic, and the issue isn't too ideologically charged, you may have a convert.

Look for the Theory

Almost everything an Analyst says is connected to a broad theoretical base, but you'll seldom get them to admit it. Analysts think of themselves as down to earth, concrete and practical. On the surface, of course, they are. But underneath are broad theoretical models that provide a staunchness (some call it stubbornness) to a belief in their own plans of action. The more you can discover what that theory base is, the better your chances of being taken seriously. If the theory is not made clear, neither will be the discussion. Once you have surfaced the theory, *then* you can begin to influence the Analyst, not before.

Salespeople often are skilled in the technique.

SALESMAN: What do you think of our calculator?

OFFICE MANAGER: Well, I have my doubts about it.

SALESMAN: You don't like the style?

OFFICE MANAGER: That makes no difference to me.

SALESMAN: You've seen it perform, and you've admitted that it's faster than your Whitney.

OFFICE MANAGER: Well, yes. But . . .

SALESMAN: Have you used Whitneys long?

OFFICE MANAGER: Forever, and nothing but Whitneys.

SALESMAN: Why haven't you ever bought one of ours?

OFFICE MANAGER: I don't know. I've just heard things, I guess.

SALESMAN: About what? Let me guess. Service?

OFFICE MANAGER: Yes. I've always gotten good service on Whitneys, but I've heard stories, you know.

SALESMAN: So that's it. You've heard that our brand is good, but not so good on service. So that's your view of it, right?

OFFICE MANAGER: That's right.

Now the salesman knows what data are needed, in great quantity. If he is persistent enough he may even make a sale. But what was needed first was uncovering that bothersome theory that was getting in the way of the influencing process.

And the word "theory" says something about Analysts that we need to remember. They are thoughtful, careful people, by and large. They don't jump to conclusions, and they usually have thoughtful reasons for believing whatever they believe.

HOW TO BE STRAIGHT-ARROW—INFLUENCING REALISTS

Any Realist will tell you there is no one more easy to connect with, no one easier to influence, provided you know what you're talking about, than the Realist. Realists are just "there," they will tell you, and all you have to do is be "there" too—wherever that is.

They are probably right.

Because Realists are relatively easy to get to, we will spend less time and space talking about Realist-influencing than that of the other Styles. That is, we'll just give you the facts.

The problem with Realists is getting their attention. They can be so focused on the reality of the moment that they can't see anything else. And what they can't see is most likely to be *your* reality.

Most of the techniques that we advocate for influencing Realists have to do with getting their attention. Here are a few of them.

Get to the Point, Quickly

We shall illustrate this technique by giving an example of its opposite in action:

Tom, the master sergeant in charge of the motor pool, has been concerned for some weeks with the behavior of some of his troops. They come to work late, they disappear for hours at a time. They always seem to have excuses. Tom, a soft-hearted fellow, can't seem to get anywhere with his usual persuasive, nice-guy tactics. At last, in desperation, he goes in to see Major Hooper, his company commander.

HOOPER: Come in, Tom. At ease and sit down. What's on your mind?

TOM: Thank you, sir. Thank you very much. Nice day, isn't it, sir?

HOOPER: Sure is. What's up, Tom?

TOM: Well— Oh, mind if I smoke, sir?

HOOPER: Help yourself.

TOM (lighting up and sighing): Ah, it's sure nice to relax for a minute.

HOOPER (drumming his fingers on the desk): Uh-huh.

TOM: Say, I hear that Captain Hickle from the 2178th is transferring out next week.

HOOPER (grimly): That's what I hear too.

TOM: Nice guy, that Captain Hickle. We'll miss him around here.

HOOPER: Yes, Tom. Tom, what's on your mind?

TOM: Oh, yes sir. Well, sir, I've been wondering for some time—

HOOPER: Yes?

TOM: And thinking about whether I ought to bother you with it and all, you being a busy man, and, uh—

HOOPER: Yes? Yes?

TOM: Well sir, you see, Major Hooper, I have this friend, this other master sergeant, and he asked me a while ago if I knew someone who might help him with his problem, and I said, "Well, sir, how about my Major Hooper," and—

HOOPER: Tom!

TOM: Yes, sir?

HOOPER: This is your last chance. Tell me what your point is in the next fifteen seconds or get the hell out of here!

Realists may only look like busy people to you, but to Realists, they *are* busy. They always have projects going, things that have to get done. They have time for small talk only when it is to the point. They simply can't be bothered with peripheral trivia, and they hate it when people beat around the bush.

While beating around the bush may be a pleasant thing to do with Idealists (sometimes they enjoy helping you get to the point), and a comforting, ritualistic pastime for certain Analysts, avoid it with Realists, if you know what's good for you.

State your case, say what you have to say, and let the chips fall where they may. You will get the attention of Realists that way, and they are likely to respect you for it.

Be Concise

Analysts sometimes have a hard time with Realists, especially when the latter are their bosses. Here is a disgruntled Realist department director, complaining about one of his senior staff:

> I'm getting to the point where I can't stand it anymore. That long-winded bastard comes in with what for anyone else would be a simple request. Well, first he gives me his life history, then he tells me what everybody in his division thinks about the thing. He gives me the pros and cons, the ins and outs, on and on. Alternatives and assessments from here to breakfast. It takes the idiot half an hour to tell me what any normal person could say in two minutes. Honest to God, one of these days I'm going to put an alarm chronometer on my desk when he comes in, and if he hasn't said his piece by the time the bell rings I'm gonna kick him bodily out of the room.

When it comes to influencing Realists, *be concise.* Say less than you think is absolutely necessary. If you are bringing in a project proposal, add a cover sheet with the meat of it crammed into two, no more than three, paragraphs. Remember, Realists often stop listening as soon as they've made a judgment, good or bad, about whatever is being told to them. If you don't get to the point fast, you may never have the chance.

"Firm but Fair"

A young man, trying to sell insurance, went into the office of a machine shop owner and delivered his spiel. The machine shop owner said, "Your argument is sound." Whereupon the young man brightened up greatly, anticipating a sale. "*All* sound," the man added. The young insurance salesman slunk away, destroyed by the aggressive humor of a Realist.

Realist managers are particularly fond of giving a hard time to visiting young staff people from headquarters. The latter, everyone knows, are full of impractical theories and cause nothing but trouble anyway.

"Nice to see you," the branch manager says. "I've got two minutes."

Such stratagems, with which Realists are adept and in the use of which they have few compunctions, call for a specific technique on the part of the potential victim.

"Nice to see you. I've got two minutes."

"I'm sorry, Mr. Baker. But when I called for an appointment the other day I said I'd need a half hour, and I do. In my opinion this is important company business, so I'd like to get to it."

The technique is particularly difficult for Idealists, who are easily bowled over by Realist assertiveness. For them it may involve an act of deliberate preliminary loin-girding, even rehearsing some lines in front of a mirror. What they discover, after a few successful experiences, is that it is the only way to get a Realist to acknowledge you, much less listen to you or give you what you came after.

Realists tend to respect only people like themselves—who seem to know what they are doing, are forthright, and stand up for themselves. They have little respect for those who are "namby-pamby" or long-winded or unsure of themselves. Hang in there until you get the Realist's attention. Once you've crossed that first major hurdle, you'll be surprised how smooth things can be.

Encourage Appropriation

Because Realists are immediate and empirical and rely so much on expert opinion they can seem very unoriginal in their thinking. They do, however, recognize a good idea when they see one.

If you are interested in influencing a Realist, this is an important thing to remember: Pride of authorship will guarantee frustration. It is amazing how "My friend Sam here had an idea the other day," can change to "You'll love this brilliant idea of mine," in the space of a few minutes.

Realists are notorious appropriators. It is an innocent act on their part. They don't willfully borrow or plagiarize. When they see something good they simply suck it up, empirically. Because everything in the world is a *fact*, a thing in itself, it simply doesn't enter the Realist's head to consider the possible connection between the thing and its originator.

Both of our wives, for instance, are constantly making off with clipboards, staplers, and other vital paraphernalia from our inner sanctums. Those necessities, to them, are *things* that are needed at the moment. That they don't return them is mere oversight, being immersed as they are in projects that have to get done. We used to rant and rage and threaten. Now we simply, patiently track things down as needed and reappropriate them. There is no use getting personal about it.

If you want to influence a Realist to buy your idea, and you want something to happen to it, encourage appropriation. Take advantage of all that energy turned loose and ride its coattails. Time enough after things have been set in motion to remind the Realist of your "contribution."

Give Control

If you are a consultant, or a therapist, or a subordinate, or a partner, or anything else vis-à-vis a Realist, do the best you can to let them have a sense of control over the situation.

Here are some examples of how to do it.

"I think we ought to do this and this and perhaps after that, this. But it depends, of course, on how you feel about it."

"I'll take responsibility for setting up the meeting, but I'll make sure to let you know how everyone responded a couple of hours beforehand."

"Just before it's time for a vote, I'll see that you get some time at the mike."

If you are working with a Realist, and you have the slightest sense that your partner feels things are getting out of hand, check it out. Ask the question directly: "Is everything okay with you?" Realists are seldom shy about letting you know, though you may not like the answer.

The worst thing you can do with Realists is put them in a situation where they feel they have lost control—to put them in a dependent position. Similarly, it is seldom productive to put yourself in a position of abject dependence on them. If you are in that state, they simply won't respect you.

If your boss is a Realist, beat the bad news to the punch. Give regular, brief reports on sensitive situations. If ever the boss gets a negative report from someone else first the reaction will hit you hard and fast. Anything you say afterward will be treated with suspicion. Don't be shy about letting Realists know where you stand. They will respect you for it.

DON'T KNOCK OPPORTUNITY— INFLUENCING PRAGMATISTS

Pragmatists are the easiest people in the world to influence. They are also the most fun to influence, if you are willing to have fun, and you are amenable to that old Pragmatist philosophy, "Win a few, lose a few."

This is the danger with Pragmatists: If you take *yourself* too seriously, Pragmatists won't take *you* seriously. In fact, they are likely to give you a wide berth. And there goes your effort at influencing.

Try to see it through Pragmatist eyes. As a Pragmatist, I *know* that the world is a piecemeal, experimental, contingent affair. I have found over the years that the way to get things done is through a bit here and a piece there. I have found satisfaction in proceeding in that way and I feel generally good about the whole thing. Why, then, should I get all solemn about this great, idealistic, world-changing plan of yours? How can I be anything but amused by your comprehensive, bulky, totally structured scheme that you guarantee will make everything work perfectly by the numbers?

When a Pragmatist looks at an Idealist's utopian concept or an Analyst's comprehensive plan, it is likely to be seen as one of those contraptions from a Rube Goldberg cartoon—amusing, but hardly to be taken seriously.

The cardinal rule for influencing a Pragmatist is this: *Don't be heavy*. Avoid a weighty tone either in the substance of what you propose, or in your presentation of yourself. What follows from that rule is precisely what has to be said about influencing any Style of Thinking. If you want to influence a Pragmatist, be like a Pragmatist. Be incremental, experimental, step lightly, and try to be a bit playful.

Bargain, Always Bargain

We have a friend in East Africa who, if he isn't a born Pragmatist himself, lives a life that calls for it as the predominant style. Gene works for an international organization. He operates what is called an Appropriate Technology Center a few miles outside of Nairobi, Kenya. There he and a few African associates design, build, and experiment with such things as backyard ovens, kilns, vegetable dryers, and waterwheels. Everything is invented on the spot, and made by hand from native materials.

The whole operation is experimental, with the objective being to develop technology that African farmers and villagers can build and operate themselves. Every development is piecemeal. The governing philosophy of the center is "Whatever works."

Once a new piece of equipment has been tested and found workable, Gene's job is to go into the bush and try to get it installed. He travels into the villages to look for African farmers and artisans who will learn how to build and operate his inventions.

What Gene is offering is designed to make the lives of these villagers easier and more productive. So you would think they would recognize the benefit, and once having seen the virtues of the technology they would buy it just like that, or at least would be eager to learn how to produce it themselves. But Gene knows perfectly well that, no matter how beneficial his inventions might be, they will not be accepted and adopted without a good deal of bargaining.

It is a way of life with the people he deals with, and with which Gene is comfortable. And he happens to think it is great fun.

Pragmatists understand the notion of trade-offs. No matter how useful or attractive your idea might be, the Pragmatist whom you are trying to influence toward accepting it understands that a price will be paid in time, energy, the sacrifice of some other interesting activity, or whatever. So let's put the chips on the table and see what they're worth to both of us.

Be prepared to bargain cheerfully with the Pragmatist. It's part of the game.

Let 'Em Be Likable

When you are trying to influence someone—anyone—there are three simple but important things to watch out for. Never threaten the other person's:

—Sense of importance.
—Sense of competence.
—Sense of being likable.

The last is especially important when you are dealing with Pragmatists. If you want a sure way of cutting off the influencing process with Pragmatists, do something to make them think you think they're not likable. They will immediately tune you out, as if you no longer exist.

Pragmatists are similar to Idealists in one respect. Both have a hard time letting you know their concerns, criticisms, or negative opinions of you or your ideas. If you want candidness from them they both need to be helped, and in similar ways. Their differences lie in *why* they always need to be so positive and pleasant.

Idealists, as we have seen, find criticism hard to deliver because they don't want to hurt your feelings and be seen as negative. Pragmatists avoid giving criticism because they want to be liked or, at least, accepted and approved.

As with Idealists, to get Pragmatists to reveal their true feelings and opinions you must explicitly invite them to do so. Here are a few likely phrases:

"Okay, what flaws have you seen in this part of the plan?" (not as a challenge, but lightly).

"If you were in my shoes, how would you go about it?" (hooks a Pragmatist's secret criticism *and* gets his or her constructive ideas).

"Which do you think are the strongest and weakest parts of my plan?"

Pick Up on the "Messages"

This technique is closely related to the preceding one. When

Pragmatists have something less than complimentary on their minds, they will often disguise it in a cloak of good humor or friendly, joking "messages."

Hubie, the vice-president for sales, meets Phil, the production manager, in the hallway.

"Phil, you old rascal," Hubie says jovially, "had any more disasters lately?"

Phil smiles and chuckles. "Not that you'd notice, Hube." They go on their way.

But Phil is a thoughtful fellow, and he knows something of Hubie's ways. When he gets back to his office he sits down and thinks about it for a moment. What might Hubie have meant by "had any more disasters lately?" Phil is not feeling defensive or paranoid, he simply understands that there is likely to be a "message" there, something beneath the humor to which he should pay attention. He also knows that one doesn't confront Hubie and ask for an explanation. Hubie would just laugh it off or worry that Phil's feelings had been hurt.

At last Phil thinks he has it. He picks up the phone and dials the vice-president.

"Hubie? It just occurred to me that you might be curious why that shipment to Chicago was twenty percent short last week—you know, when your salesmen out there took so much heat. Did you hear that our strut supplier shorted us two weeks before? It seems no one over in Purchasing caught it at the time and we didn't doublecheck. We've tightened our own control system as a result. I thought you might like to know."

To which Hubie responds: "Say, thanks for telling me, Phil. As a matter of fact, I was a little curious about that. Just hadn't got around to asking you. Yeah, thanks—I appreciate it."

By being sensitive to a possible "message" in Hubie's humor, Phil has been able to protect his own rear and preserve his image

of a careful problem-solving manager. More importantly, he resolved a doubt in Hubie's mind that might have caused trouble
later.

Take a Marketing Stance

Pragmatists understand the value of a quid pro quo approach to
life. They like selling to others and they enjoy being sold. What
leaves them feeling helplessly frustrated is encountering someone
who seems immune to negotiation, bargaining, and a search for
mutually beneficial trade-offs.

Marcia, a fund raiser, was hired to develop a plan and program
for a new community organization. The organization was made
up entirely of women, who had made a solemn pact that they
would organize and manage themselves entirely along humane,
non-exploitive lines. They resolved that the way businesses were
run by men (as they understood it) would not be their way.

Marcia spent some time getting familiar with the organization
and its members. Then she held a meeting. She said to them:
"You do a fine job of doing what you say you are doing. You are
professionals in your field. You manage your operations remarkably well. The only thing you don't do well is raise money. What
that calls for is marketing skills. It would be prohibitively expen-
sive to have me do it for you, but you don't need that anyway,
you have the talent right here in your own group."

To that one young woman responded with enthusiasm: "That's
just what Paula and I have been trying to tell the rest of you for a
year! We'd both love to go out after capital if the rest of you
would only see that it's okay."

There followed a lengthy and rather solemn discussion, the gist
of which was, "But would that be nice?" (the group was loaded
with Idealists). And "Would that go against our principles?"

Then Marcia said, "You have a pretty clear choice, it seems to
me. Either you do good works and go slowly broke, or you go after
money and do good works even better."

Thus the two young women were unleashed to perform the
Pragmatist acts of fund raising and marketing. In a struggling
community agency the Pragmatist approach is really the only way
to go.

When influencing people whom you have reason to believe are Pragmatists, dismiss any compunctions you may have about selling or marketing. "Have I got a deal for you," with a twinkle in your voice, is not a bad opening.

Innovative, experimental Pragmatists are open to new things and new ideas. They understand that the world is largely a marketplace. They have a feeling for what will sell and what people will buy, and they don't mind at all being sold. "What's it good for?" is their question.

So show them!

The Win-Win Compromise

The delightful thing about Pragmatists is that they never expect to get everything they want. The frustrating thing about them is that they know you aren't going to get everything you want, either. For them, finding the productive middle ground between the two is a fascinating game.

This is not to say that for Pragmatists life is all a game. They can be just as serious as any of us in their private moments. But in the public world where influencing has to be done, they feel, why not relax a little and enjoy the whole thing? If the world is contingent, then so am I. What sense does it make to be solemn about whether I achieve this or fail to achieve that? It is so much a matter of serendipity, anyhow.

Given that point of view, only compromise makes sense. And Win-Win Compromise is the most appealing game of all. Here is an example.

Lee was corporate training director and Darrell was personnel manager. Lee was new in his job. Darrell had been in his for several years. For the first year in his new position, Lee became increasingly puzzled over what he saw as Darrell's obstructionism, his subtle opposition to Lee's plans.

In order for people to be interested in his work, Lee needed Darrell's support. Specifically, he needed personnel policies that would encourage people and make it easier for them to attend his training programs. But help from Darrell never seemed to be forthcoming, no matter how friendly he seemed and how agreeable he was in their meetings.

One day Lee took the initiative and went to Darrell's office.

"Look, Darrell," he said, "in order to make my operation a success I need certain things from you. I think you know that."

"Yep," Darrell said. "I know that."

"It occurs to me that I've never asked you what you might want or need from me. I'm here to ask you, so that maybe we might work up a mutually productive arrangement."

Darrell's eyes brightened. "Okay. I'll tell you. I've been in this job for five years, and what I want is to be promoted out as soon as possible."

"And?"

"And to do that I need more recognition. I need people in the company to see all the good things we're doing in Personnel."

"I think I begin to get a glimmering," Lee said. "Right now I'm getting all the attention."

"That's about it."

"So what can we do about that?"

"I'll tell you what I'd like," Darrell said. "You know all those courses you're doing in Personnel Practices?"

"Yes."

"Let me develop them, run them, and promote them, under Personnel's name. We'll do them in your facility, of course."

"Will that do it?" Lee asked.

"Well, it would be helpful if we were to co-sponsor more courses."

"Done," Lee said. "And in return?"

"I'll see to it that your other programs are filled to the brim."

"Done and done," Lee said, shaking hands with his former antagonist.

Lee had come to understand that Darrell would never force a confrontation. Lee also guessed that Darrell might be open to compromise. He was right, and it was a thoroughly successful influencing effort.

Six months later Darrell was promoted to director of administrative services. His first real act in his new job was to suggest to Lee, now his subordinate, that perhaps the training department needed to expand its services and, of course, Lee's budget.

We said at the beginning of this section that Pragmatists are the easiest of all to influence, provided you choose the right approach. Another nice thing about them is that influencing them doesn't take long when it works. The frequently quick, to-the-point nature of dealing with Pragmatists can be one of the most refreshing aspects of the whole business of influencing people.

Life is not only contingent but short, and Pragmatists seem to have a healthy grasp of that reality.

THE MEDIUM IS THE MESSAGE— INFLUENCING SYNTHESISTS

Frankly, we doubt that it is possible to do much in the way of influencing Synthesists under any circumstances.

It all depends, we suppose, on what you mean by "influencing." If by influencing you mean "convincing," then when it comes to Synthesists there is only one thing to say: Forget it! To convince a Synthesist of anything for any length of time is a logical impossibility, a contradiction in terms. Because what makes the most sense to Synthesists is *contradiction itself*. You might "convince" a Synthesist of something right now, but five minutes later he or she can be heartily embracing the opposite.

How about "persuading," then? Well, maybe, but with similar reservations. It is terribly hard to persuade a Synthesist of anything, because of that Synthesist penchant for creating new ideas. Synthesists have a burning need to discover things for themselves. Sometimes it becomes tiresome, in that they are constantly, with great delight, reinventing the wheel. But after all that's their problem.

You might very well think, then, that the basic problem with Synthesists is one of ego. Certainly the Synthesists we know aren't terribly strong on humility. However, it is just a matter of that peculiar worldview of theirs, a basic belief that life is change, newness, the process of becoming. If I am a Synthesist, you are most likely to influence me if you have an interesting new opposite up your sleeve. Otherwise, I've forgotten you already.

We have observed a few Synthesist-influencing techniques. Remember, while they are practical and they work much of the time, they are not at all guaranteed to last.

The Cajoling Specific

This technique is applicable to a Synthesist boss, when it is necessary to make some practical sense out of his or her high-flown generalities. It is also useful with a Synthesist spouse, when for once you would really like to say something specific about what we might do next week or next year, instead of just speculating about it.

Here is what a boss might say:

> "The fascinating thing about what we are doing here is that we're in an existentially absurd situation. On the one hand, we can reasonably anticipate a potentially enormous demand for our services. On the other hand, we have no good identification of our public, and we're not even sure that our public, if there is one, is aware of our existence. What if, for instance, next week we were all to disappear in some great earthquake? Who would know? Or care? That's the interesting question."

To which you reply:

> "Yes, indeed. I think that may be an important question. And our quarterly report is due next week, which I've been working on. How might we phrase the question so those people upstairs could understand it?"

If you are lucky, you may actually get the Synthesist to get specific. The trick is to get him or her to see it as a temporarily interesting challenge.

Realists probably have the strongest potential for bringing Synthesists down to earth, if they have the patience to stick with it. "Can you give me an example of that?" "What would that look like?" "How would we say that in the report?"

The technique, in a nutshell, is to cajole Synthesists into getting specific by making them think it is worth their while to do so.

"Don't Bother Me with Facts"

Synthesists love to speculate and hypothesize, theorize, and throw around ideas, play with contradictions. Sometimes it is fruitless to try to bring them down to earth. Let them have their fun.

The point here is twofold:

> 1. Out of all that speculation, etc., may come some really useful ideas, if you can only listen for them ("Out of the mouths of babes," as it were . . .).
> 2. It is up to you to take the responsibility for finding the practical applications in that welter of confusion.

What that means is that to a considerable extent you have to suspend your own practical judgment, your own sober, structured rationality, and just concentrate on *listening* to all the blather. At least, Synthesists will appreciate your attention.

Fighting Can Be Fun

Here is John, a salesman of office equipment, calling on Jessica, administrative manager for a large engineering firm. Listen to a portion of their conversation:

> JESSICA: I don't know what you guys think you're doing. Here you just came out a few months ago with the most space-age typewriter in existence, and now you say you've got something even better. Are you trying to kid me?
> JOHN: It's called planned obsolescence.
> JESSICA: That's what I thought.
> JOHN: Or the knowledge explosion. Take your choice.
> JESSICA: Oh sure! And it makes you a fat lot of money, right?
> JOHN: You bet. And just what do you think you're up to here?
> JESSICA: Making a fat lot of money. What else?
> JOHN: So together we could be dynamite.

JESSICA: Look. Suppose we bought your new gadget. How long would it be till you were back here telling me it's outmoded?

JOHN: Just as soon as possible.

JESSICA: I suppose you give a good trade-in allowance?

JOHN: None at all. That's how you get a chance to contribute to your favorite charity.

JESSICA: Sometimes I wonder if people like you know what you're doing.

JOHN: I suppose you do.

JESSICA: Listen, wise guy. We build power plants and generators. Monster ones.

JOHN: Big deal. What does that prove?

JESSICA: Have you ever heard of one of our plants blowing up?

JOHN: No, but how much news do we ever hear from Iceland or Upper Volta?

And so forth. What is going on here is two people having fun and influencing each other famously. Confronted by Jessica's immediate sardonic challenge, John knew exactly how to respond. He threw back the challenge, mobilized his wit, and let the encounter build. As the exchange escalates, it might sound to some as if it will wind up in outright warfare. How could Jessica waste her time with this nonsense? Can't John see that he is blowing any chance he might have had to do business here?

Quite the contrary. These two Synthesists, through their matching of wits, are building a relationship. Chances are John will do a handsome amount of business. And he would have gotten nowhere by becoming defensive or apologetic.

Sparring, teasing, matching wits, the friendly fight: this is one of the best ways to influence a Synthesist for the short term. But it's hard work if you're not used to it.

"Which Way Did It Go?"

The history of scientific discovery is replete with accounts of profound insights that took place unconsciously, during a period of fantasy, or arose from tangents that seemed to have nothing to do with the problem at hand.

A fascinating example is the story of the discovery of the DNA molecule. F. H. C. Crick and J. D. Watson had been struggling for a long time trying to isolate DNA, but their conscious efforts were to no avail. One night, in a dream or semidream, one of them envisioned the figure of connected spirals—the double helix. It was a visual, graphic tangent that led to the conceptualization and eventual discovery of the long-sought molecule.

Synthesists are especially prone to blurting out fresh ideas and insights in ways that seem to have no relevance to the matter at hand. Most people—intent on and serious about their problem—tend to pay no attention, and the potentially fruitful solution is lost forever.

Seriously, Play Around a Lot

Given the Synthesist's speculative, "What if," sometimes far-out orientation toward problem solving, a valuable form of influencing is to find a way to capture the products of the Synthesist's unconventional and nonlinear thinking.

What that calls for is a commitment, now and then, to data-gathering approaches that are unstructured, free-form, and that permit playfulness with ideas. One of the best ways we know to go about that is what is called "brainstorming." The ground rules for brainstorming have been written a thousand times, and usually go like this:

1. Every idea is acceptable (even if it sounds silly).
2. No evaluation of ideas is permitted during the brainstorming period, either verbal or nonverbal approval or disapproval.
3. The quantity of ideas is the main goal—quality ideas will normally follow. This is called freewheeling.
4. Building on the contributions of others is referred to as hitchhiking and is encouraged.
5. Group members should be encouraged to think of "opposites" to ideas that have already been suggested.[2]

[2] This version of the rules of brainstorming is adapted from Neely D. Gardner, *Group Leadership* (Washington, D.C.: NTDS Press, 1974), p. 100.

It should be clear from this outline that brainstorming is a natural for the Synthesist mind. Given the right players, brainstorming is the most efficient way we know of gathering original and creative ideas from a group of people.

The trouble with brainstorming is that there are so few Synthesists in any group, and not many more Pragmatists, who are likely players too. Almost everyone else finds the technique artificial, tedious, or generally unbearable. Analysts can't understand how you can have "opposites" to perfectly sensible ideas. Realists see irrelevancy and "silliness" as just that, with no value. Idealists can't restrain themselves from evaluating ideas against their own high standards and ideals—especially those Synthesist ideas that seem impudent or irreverent.

Our experience has been that brainstorming is a useful technique for influencing Synthesists to contribute new and useful ideas.

Influencing or Manipulating?

At this point we can pretty well predict the reactions of those of you who have come this far with us. We suspect you fall, with some overlap, into three fairly distinct points of view.

There will be those who are more amused than anything else by what we have discussed in this chapter. You will have found some useful ideas, will acknowledge that we have struck home now and then, but primarily you were entertained.

A second group of you will be intrigued by the clear practicality of a number of the techniques. You will have begun already (at least in your mind's eye) to experiment with some of our influencing methods.

A third, rather sizable group may be both entertained and intrigued by the potential usefulness of the influencing techniques, but one overriding question nags at you: Isn't all of this just a grand scheme for manipulating people?

The answer, of course, is emphatically *Yes!* And our question in response is, "What's so bad about that?"

For, if manipulating means doing things in a purposive and intentional way, we manipulate others every day of our lives. We call it influencing or persuading or making a connection. In that sense we manipulate our children so that they will grow up the way we want them to. We manipulate our spouses or lovers so that they will love us more, and love us as we would be loved. We manipulate bosses in order to get promoted. We do things with and for our friends so that they will continue to be our friends. It is for this reason that those occasional intimate and truly spontaneous moments with friends or family are so cherished and remembered.

We suggest that the real questions to be asked are these:

1. Are we doing what we're doing for good purposes? (Of course we are! We're all honorable people.)

2. If we were to let those others in on what we were doing and why, would they feel mistreated or would they feel acknowledged and understood?

3. Are we doing what we're doing knowledgeably and with awareness of the consequences, for ourselves and others?

To manipulate clumsily and unconsciously, without competence, is one thing. To do so knowledgeably and competently is another.

Manipulation, as we see it, is just another term for *application of method*. The techniques for influencing that we have described in this chapter—sometimes seriously, sometimes more or less facetiously—are methods for improving your interactions with other people. It seems to us that the well-intentioned, and enlightened use of method in human relations can only be a good thing.

From our point of view, the conscious, skillful use of influencing techniques is a productive use of individual talents and strengths. And that, from another direction and in more detail, is the subject of our next chapter.

Chapter X

THE PRODUCTIVE USE OF
YOUR STRENGTHS

On Not Being Ashamed of Yourself

Nobody's perfect.

Every one of us is a bewildering mixture of strength and weakness, assets and liabilities, skill and clumsiness, excellence and mediocrity. One of life's brightest moments comes when we realize that although we aren't perfect, we don't have to be.

This is not one of those books that tries to tell you that you've already got it, whatever "it" is, and that all you have to do is unleash your hidden powers and you will rule the universe.

Our aims are much more modest. We think you are probably just as fallible as we are. At times we are woefully inept, and we suspect you are too. But at other times we are amazed by our own excellence, and that, we find, is a pleasant, exhilarating experience. We do think that a reasonable goal for most people is to increase the frequency of those moments of justified self-satisfaction. An enlightened understanding of your Style of Thinking, and a more skillful use of existing talents and strengths can do just that.

The first step in doing that is to stop wishing you were different. Even though the I_nQ is focused less on personality and more on cognitive behavior, it can draw out the self-doubting worries of many people.

Here are some of the questions that we have heard:

"What's the best combination of Styles of Thinking to have?"

"Is it neurotic to have high scores at opposite ends of the I_nQ scale?"

"Is it possible to have too much of one Style?"

Or, even more frequently:

"I don't like my profile. I wish I had more (or less) . . . [take your choice of any other Style of Thinking]."

To each of these worried questions, and especially to those wishing more openly to be different, we give the same answer: Every Style of Thinking, every combination, has its strengths and its inseparable liabilities. They are inseparable because the weaknesses are usually nothing more than strengths used too much or in the wrong place. That sort of inconsistency is what makes us people, not machines, and therefore fascinating.

In the brief survey to follow, we shall take another look at each Style of Thinking. We'll give examples of the kinds of situations in which each Style of Thinking is normally at its best and strongest, and we'll give some suggestions on (a) how to recognize those situations, and (b) how to mobilize the appropriate strengths for the situation.

If you have a combination of Style of Thinking preferences, remember the "salt and pepper" analogy. Confronted by a situation calling for salt, bring out your *best* salt. If it's a pepper situation, choose accordingly. Modify one with the other, according to taste and the needs of the moment.

You begin to really use those unique qualities of mind that are your strengths when you have learned to respect them as strengths. It is quite understandable to find yourself worrying about having too much of this or too little of that. It is understandable and most human, but not very constructive. Our advice for the moment, therefore, is: Knock it off! Life is a matter of choices, and the first, most basic choice, is to do the best with the equipment you already have.

THE SYNTHESIST AS HERO OR HEROINE

Synthesist strengths are at their best in situations that are unstructured, unclear, laden with values, and potential conflict. This is where incisiveness is of value, together with a relatively high tolerance for ambiguity. In other words, "The Mind-Boggling Mess" is the kind of situation in which Synthesists are likely to be more effective than anyone else.

Idealists and Analysts, of course, might refer to that sort of thing as "Fools rush in. . . ." But let's look at some examples.

The Analyst of Conflict

Once we were called into an organization by its manager at a critical point. The manager said that the clerical staff and their supervisor were locked in mortal combat. Fear and loathing were so advanced on both sides, he said, that to have a consultant come in was clearly a last-ditch effort, but it was the only recourse left. Could we resolve the situation somehow?

When we talked individually with the supervisor and each of the six clerks, we discovered the situation to be just as the manager had described it. It seemed clear to us that the supervisor was a highly disturbed person—for whatever reasons, she was tyrannical, and utterly unpleasant. Her behavior had so affected the other women that they were unanimously adamant about refusing to cooperate with her anymore. Either she left or they would.

After all the interviews were completed, we called a meeting of the group. The six clerks filed in and sat on one side of the room. The supervisor sat on the other. The battle lines were clearly drawn. We decided it was time for what we privately termed the "Dutch uncle" treatment. We delivered a short speech:

> "I have put the issues up here on the blackboard, as I heard them from both sides. It may be possible to learn how to work together. It may not. I suggest you have two choices: either make some agreements to work cooperatively, or call it quits."

After a half hour of discussion, part of which consisted of half-hearted attempts by Idealists in the group to look for points of hopeful agreement, but which was mostly a repetition of old accusations, the meeting ended suddenly when the supervisor got up, announced her resignation, and left the room. It seemed clear to us that it was the only solution under the circumstances.

We sometimes pride ourselves, in our organizations, on the Idealist ability to "resolve conflict." Often, this means compromising value questions that should be boldly faced. Then, the best resolution is to get it over with, to end drawn-out, deep but covert strug-

STYLES OF THINKING

134

gles. Synthesist approaches are the method of choice in such situations. The Synthesist becomes "analyst," making the conflict clear and dispassionately presenting the choices to the combatants.

Forcing the Hard Choices

This example goes a little beyond the preceding one. We think of a family, in which the young son, otherwise well-behaved if somewhat irresponsible, has been caught shoplifting for the third time. Each previous time he has excused himself by saying that one of his friends "talked him into it." Each time his Idealist, supportive mother tried to counsel him, but to no avail.

This time, the father takes the boy off for a chat.

> "Three times is enough. The next time, I am assured by the police, it will be juvenile hall for you. You can no longer blame your actions on others. It is your responsibility alone. What's your decision?"

Confronted by the hard choices of the Synthesist father, the boy never shoplifted again.

These examples share certain characteristics: The situation is complex, unclear, involves weighty choices, and appears to the actors more of a "mess" than a well-defined problem. The Synthesist's willingness to clarify the situation by confronting the conflict—sometimes unfeelingly, always boldly and incisively—is of enormous value.

Synthesists often feel uncomfortable with themselves, as they feel the power of this strength—the ability to see contradiction, to recognize conflict, and to confront it when others shy away. It is difficult to cherish a gift that sets a person off from others. But it is the Synthesist gift, and a rare one—it needs to be cultivated and sharpened. Along with the ability to see the absurdity in serious things (which we know also to be uncomfortable at times), it is the source of Synthesist power.

THE IDEALIST AS SAVIOR

An exciting book, called *Alive,* is an account of a Uruguayan soccer team whose airplane went down in the Andes a number of years ago, and the team was marooned in the snow for the winter. Aside from the bizarre component of cannibalism, the story is compelling from the point of view of group behavior and the phenomenon of leadership.

During their gruesome ordeal, the survivors of the crash divided spontaneously into three groups. There was a group of three or four "movers," the strongest physically of them all, characterized by their energy and impatience; there was another group of three, who were characterized by their calmness, their willingness to be patient, and their desire to watch out for the welfare of the whole community; the rest fell into the general category of followers, who went along with whatever the leadership directed and who performed the routine work of survival.

The movers wanted to save the group by hiking out of the mountains for help, immediately. They seized leadership of the community at the start. But weather conditions were hideous. The movers made an attempt to get out, lost one of their number in a blizzard, and barely made it back to the wrecked plane.

At that point, the quiet leadership took over. They convinced the movers that they must wait until the winter was over to perform their rescue. Meanwhile the community must organize itself in order to survive over the next couple of months, and the move when it took place must be well-planned. In the meantime, recognizing that the movers were indeed the strongest and most capable of saving them all, they were to be relatively pampered, given the best food, relieved of routine duties, and kept in training for the eventual rescue. The quiet leaders prevailed.

When the bad weather ended, most of the crash survivors were still alive, and the movers were strong and ready. They made it out, down the mountain, and arranged the rescue of their friends. Of course they were hailed publicly as the heroes of the tale by the outside world. But if it hadn't been for the strength and endurance of the quiet leadership, no one would have survived. Theirs we identify as an example of what we call:

The Nurturing Sensibility

It is perhaps the greatest strength of the Idealist. And although the word "nurturing" is often used as a feminine characteristic, we know it is just as common to men. More appropriately, it is an Idealist characteristic, and equally common to males and females of that persuasion.

Those who nurture are seldom heroes. They are seldom acclaimed. They are instead the ones who calmly (and hopefully) maintain the psychological strength of the group, who help others out and quietly support the movement of people toward their goal.

Nurturing is not dramatic, or flashy, and nurturers are not often seen as charismatic, but they have a profound strengthening effect on others. They are seen as people upon whom one can depend. It is especially important in our society that Idealists see that as a strength, and nurture their own skills in nurturing.

When Overall Goals Are Essential

One of us was called in to work with an interdisciplinary scientific team at a university. There were about fifteen scientists, each from a separate discipline or specialty. Each was an eminent researcher; each was highly specialized.

Now, as people with experience in academia know, many research scientists are not accustomed to working in teams. For example, in the highly specialized world of biological research, it is normal to focus on your own specialty, to work alone or with assistants as specialized as yourself, to publish your findings independently. Even the reward system punishes teamwork. Promotion and collegial respect elude those whose publications all have had several authors.

To put fifteen such people together and tell them to work as a team, then, goes against the grain of their professional life. Yet it was essential, in order for the project to succeed, that the scientists work and think together, coordinate their activities, and communicate openly with each other.

Two mechanisms were used to accomplish this feat. One was analytical, and of immediate appeal to the mostly Analyst scientists. A complex system was designed, in the form of a great project planning chart that showed how each separate research question fitted into the whole, specified what needed to be known in order to proceed, and just exactly how the work of each scientist would interface with the others and with the overall outcome of the project.

The second mechanism was a series of meetings. Here two things were done. First, the scientists were split up into groups and assigned the task of defining the overall goal of the project, and how each person's part of it fit into the overall picture. The groups then reported to each other informally, and discussed their separate views until some agreement had been reached on their mutual goal. Second, each small group was asked to invent ways for making sure that data were shared as the project moved along. What resulted from this step was a number of informal agreements between people, about when and how they would get together and share ideas.

The process served two functions. First, it resulted in a general agreement on goals—an "umbrella" over all the differing, specialized, and often competing scientific disciplines. Second, it led to the development of an informal, interpersonal community of effort, beyond (or beside) the formal framework, which established productive relationships on a personal as well as a professional level.

Readers will recognize a favorite Idealist strategy—an agreement on broad goals, on the overall, beneath which technical differences can be subsumed and reconciled. It is precisely in this sort of situation that Idealist strengths can be of immense value.

Supportiveness at Work (and Elsewhere)

The literature of management has put great stress the last twenty or thirty years on the notion of participation. As we have noted before, participative management is a mode that has great natural appeal to Idealists.

A particular aspect of this way of managing is what is called the "supportive relationship." Rensis Likert, an organizational scholar formerly with the University of Michigan, has identified that principle as a basic element of management. He said that the manager's ability to be supportive of others was essential to productivity. Here are his early words on the subject:

The principle of supportive relationships points to a dimension essential for the success of every organization, namely, that the mission of the organization be seen by its members as genuinely important.[1]

Supportiveness, of course, is one of the basic characteristics of the Idealist Style of Thinking. With many Idealists whom we have observed in management and other leadership positions, that characteristic takes a number of forms. Sometimes it is a kind of quiet calmness, a serenity in the face of difficulty—the Idealist as a sort of calm center of the storm. In others it appears as a subtly inspirational quality, an enduring, stable optimism that motivates others by example. And sometimes it takes the form of a faith and confidence in the members of the organization that comes across as trust.

Idealists sometimes feel put upon by their tendency to trust overmuch. They are painfully aware at times of the price they pay, often in disappointment with others, for their high standards and expectations. But they are people of good instincts. Their instincts tell them clearly when it is the time and place for nurturing, for emphasizing goals and the long range, and for fostering supportive relationships. To the extent that they respect those instincts and go with them, and avoid their overuse, Idealists use their strengths productively.

THE PRAGMATIST AS SORCERER'S APPRENTICE

Pragmatists, as we know by now, are resourceful people in an immediate, situational way—so much so, at times, that it seems a little like gilding the lily to point out to them the kinds of situations that call for their productive strengths. They seem to recognize such situations almost as a reflex action. Of all people they are probably the least inclined to agonize over whether or not their strategies are the "right" ones. They seem to engage less than others in ethical deliberation or a conscious selection process.

Here are three examples of situations that highlight Pragmatist strengths. Pragmatists will read this section and say, "Well, of course!" So maybe this is for the rest of us to learn from.

[1] Rensis Likert, *New Patterns of Management* (New York: McGraw-Hill, 1961).

"Has Anyone Got an Idea?"

One day a group of senior students in a small Midwestern college were sitting around disconsolately. It was just before the Christmas holiday, and they were depressed. There were seven young men and women, and every one of them had been turned down for graduate school. Their depression was heightened by their awareness that most of their classmates were going on to graduate school. But in another few months these young people were going to have to find jobs.

As they talked, they found that none of them knew how to go about getting a job. As liberal arts students, none were aware of what kinds of work might be open to people like themselves. None understood the first thing about the working world, though several suggested that they had better choose carefully because, they imagined, once you took a job that was it for life. With some bitterness, they commented that no one on the faculty could advise them because none of them knew anything either: all their professors had done in life was go to graduate school and teach.

What to do? Things looked bleak.

Finally someone said, "The least we need to know is how to get a job. There must be someone who can help us."

Someone else said, "Who knows anything about it?"

"Nobody here, that's for sure," one of them said gloomily.

Then Jennifer spoke up. "There are lots of people who should know."

"Who?" came the chorus.

"People who have done it," she said. "People who used to be in our position. How about alumni?"

"But they're all somewhere else. Working."

"I have an idea," Jennifer said. "The Anthropology Department, I happen to know, has six hundred dollars in uncommitted conference funds. It's just sitting there. And there must be sixty or eighty students like us, right? Well, how about an all-college senior conference in the spring?"

"On what?"

"On careers, of course. We go to the Alumni Office and get them to help us find a number of alumni who didn't go to graduate school but seem to have been successful anyhow. We use the money to pay some of their expenses so thay can come and tell us how they found jobs."

"How are you going to get the Anthro Department to spring for that?"

"Aren't we a study in human behavior? A deprived sub-culture?" Jennifer said playfully. "And isn't it true that fewer Anthro majors than anyone else got into graduate school? Why, they *owe* it to us!"

Jennifer was able to pull off her conference, and it was a resounding success. Her Pragmatist enthusiasm was the key. She had an idea, when everyone else could only worry and complain. She saw an opportunity that no one else saw. She had the imagination to see how they might innovate with what was available. And she instinctively saw the students' bargaining position with the Anthropology Department. Jennifer worked the Pragmatist's "opportunistic" magic.

Tactical Leadership

Pragmatists like to figure out how to get from here to there. They have an ability to put themselves in someone else's shoes in order to get a sense of what will work. And they are satisfied with piecemeal progress. In other words, they excel at tactical thinking. When that kind of thinking is called for in a leadership situation, it can be immensely powerful.

There is probably no more notable an example of such leadership than Saul Alinsky, the community organizer who thrived in working class areas of Chicago a few decades ago. Alinsky was a master of tactics. Without great resources, political backing or money, his impact in the community was always dramatic. One of his secrets was grass-roots organizing ability. Another was a neat ability to plot a course from where he was to where he wanted to be.

Here is an example. In order to push through a housing proposal that his group wanted to pursue with city hall, Alinsky determined that the support of the neighborhood priest was essential. The priest, doubtless for good reasons, preferred to remain neutral and "apolitical," and withheld his support despite many earnest requests from his parishioners, of whom a large number of the most influential were part of Alinsky's organization.

One day Saul made a social call on the priest. In the course of the conversation the priest mentioned that the semiannual church bingo game was coming up in a couple of weeks. Alinsky remarked that no doubt the bingo game was an important source of revenue for the parish. Indeed, the priest agreed, it was probably the biggest money raiser of all. Alinsky asked how many bingo players were expected. The priest named a number. Alinsky asked what would happen if only a third that many showed up. "Why, it would be a disaster," said the priest.

Whereupon, as you may imagine, Alinsky casually suggested to the priest how it might happen that two-thirds of his parishioners could be persuaded to stay away from the bingo game. The priest promptly gave his support to Alinsky's program.

Extortion, you say? Certainly, from one point of view. From the Pragmatist point of view, merely a negotiated, win-win compromise; though the anecdote exemplifies why others sometimes see Pragmatists as unprincipled.

Risking the Unlikely

Les, a teacher of political science, once spent a summer working with the government of a fairly small city in the Rocky Mountains. The city manager asked him to work on a problem, which was described as a growing unrest among the citizens, a general dissatisfaction with the effectiveness of city government.

Les spent some time talking to people in the city, and isolated a number of specific problem areas. One of them was the performance of the city planning department. Many citizens said that the planners were experts at "drawing pictures," that is, physical planning and design, but did nothing to coordinate what they were doing or to look ahead from development to development. The citizens complained that city planning was going on in a hit-or-miss manner.

Les got acquainted with the planning department, and determined to his own satisfaction that the citizens' complaints were justified. He arranged to have a meeting of the department. The ostensible purpose of the meeting was to "determine the goals" of the agency.

That meeting turned into a series of six sessions, during which Les trained the city planners in setting objectives, selecting alternatives, forecasting, data analysis, coordination, and a number of other things. He also taught them a good deal about public relations. At the end of the sessions several people in the group complimented Les on his teaching.

"We'll use this in the future," one of them said. "I have a feeling we aren't just going to be drawing boxes anymore."

Another one said, "The most important thing is that we've learned how to coordinate. I don't think we'll be doing our work in isolation from here on."

"Exactly," Les said. "Ladies and gentlemen, you planners have now learned something about how to plan."

Pragmatists are often blessed with a sort of matter-of-fact chutzpah. Les saw that the immediate, short-term payoff for the planning department was to become more responsive to the community and its growth. The planners needed to get out of their technical, specialized boxes. To have the audacity to teach planners how to plan is to risk the unlikely, but it worked—partly because it was done with a light touch and partly because the planners didn't know what they were learning until it had been done to them.

The great strength of Pragmatists lies in their unpretentious audacity, their playfulness, and their ability to see immediate, piecemeal opportunities where more solemn, global thinkers see so much that they become overloaded or overwhelmed. When Pragmatists feel that itchy, amusing, "Why don't we just do it" kind of enthusiasm, they need to respect it and figure out how to mobilize it. It is their special kind of magic.

THE ANALYST AS PROPHET

Analysts usually know and appreciate the power that their relentless rationality gives them. When that strength has been properly matched with situations that require it, it has moved mountains, built bridges, and designed man's path to the moon and outer space.

The problem with Analysts, perhaps more than with any other Style of Thinking, is that they simply do not recognize those situations in which their strengths are inappropriate. Analysts have such firm convictions about the necessity for method—logic, rationality, the "one best way"—that they often can't see the alternatives.

The Analyst approach has great power within a range of situations. Here are a few of them.

The Troubleshooting Detailer

Have you a brochure to publish, and you want it to be letter-perfect before you send it out into the world to display your wares? Do you have a financial report to prepare? A research paper needs editing and proofreading? Is the bridge over the creek at your acreage in need of rebuilding, and you want it designed to last forever this time? Are you planning a trip in a space ship, and you want to be sure your vehicle is put together perfectly?

Hire an Analyst.

All other things being equal (intelligence, training, technical ability, etc.), these are all tasks that call for Analyst skills—meticulousness, thoroughness, system, attention to detail, patience, orderly procedure, structured inquiry, endurance, and a kind of stolid stamina peculiar to Analysts.

And Analysts know it. That is why both Analyst parents and Analyst managers are often poor delegators. Analysts know perfectly well when those around them are slipshod, careless, and hasty. Where the situation calls for all those things mentioned in the previous paragraph, and it is essential that the result be as letter-perfect as possible, the Analyst instinct *not* to delegate is a perfectly correct one. In those situations they should stick to their guns. Those of us who know in our hearts that we are sometimes impatiently careless should let them. Analysts are their own best constructive nit-pickers; and ours too.

Step by Step by Step

Here is a practical suggestion for those of you who find yourselves in the position of applying for government grants or contracts.

You can assume that whoever wrote the Request for Proposal or the Request for Grant Application is an Analyst. What that person wants is a proposal that is laid out objectively, step-by-step, in perfect order down to the pickiest detail, and with impeccable chronological logic. If you don't know what all that means, ask an Analyst. Then ask the Analyst to translate your speculative, abstract ideas into just the proper format.

The other thing that is wanted in that proposal is perfect attention to the fiscal details. Only an Analyst can do that properly.

Analysts perform an incalculably valuable service for those of us who can't for the life of us put things together in a logical manner. In the performance of that service, the Analyst's skill must be respected. No matter that you feel you are losing the spontaneity, the spirit, the exuberance of your ideas. The people who will read your visionary prose have no patience with that sort of thing anyway. The Analyst knows that perfectly well.

Doing Things Right for a Change

Insurance company presidents, bankers, tax accountants, nuclear engineers, neurosurgeons, research chemists, radiologists, and microcomputer designers have to be people who do things right, or they aren't likely to last long. If they haven't a strong orientation to the Analyst Style of Thinking, or a close assistant who has it, they aren't likely to make it. Furthermore, they could be dangerous.

The other day one of us was at the home of an elderly gentleman who had given us a large number of boxes, cartons, and other paraphernalia that filled our van. Left over was an antique footlocker that had to ride on top. We had twenty feet of rope, with which our experienced friend proceeded to secure the locker.

We knew, from past experience, that he had pronounced Analyst characteristics. He informed us, as he manipulated the rope, that he had studied the art of knot tying in his time. He certainly had. He took fifteen minutes (we would have taken three, in our slipshod manner, and would have had to stop eight times on the way home to adjust our work), but when he was finished that footlocker couldn't move a centimeter in any direction in a high wind. It took a half hour to untie the knots at the other end.

It had no doubt been sixty years before, when our friend was a sailor, that he had studied knots. Analysts never forget. When they learn something, they learn it forever. And they do it right.

Situations such as these, calling for attention to detail, flawless linear logic, and a sort of dedicated perfectionism, are the proper arena for the use of Analyst skills. So are some other situations—

those demanding a certain stability, endurance, and a respect for the status quo.

THE REALIST AS CATALYST

Red McMurphy, hero of Ken Kesey's novel, *One Flew over the Cuckoo's Nest*, is an essential Realist. He has an amazingly incisive ability to see immediately to the gist of things, the nub. "Who's the bull-goose looney around here?" he asks forthrightly, when he first enters the mental hospital. He sees at once that the group therapy sessions in which his fellow patients indulge daily are causing them more harm than good. He says, in effect, "Why don't you just stop this nonsense?"

McMurphy calls a spade a spade wherever he sees it, as Realists are wont to do. He is an empiricist, dealing with each person's problem as he finds it. But most of all, McMurphy is a catalyst, an energizer. Because of him, the patients come alive, they begin to take responsibility for themselves, and they are moved to action. McMurphy's story is an example of the Realist skill that we call:

Energizing Organizing

Kesey was trying to tell us something about daily life and organizational life, as well as life in the "hatch." The story reminds us that too often a work group (or a family or an organization or a whole society) can become passive and without energy in the face of adversity. Here the energy and force that flow from the Realist approach can make the difference between fretful acquiescence and constructive change. Realists, of course, always take the risk that their efforts to make things happen will result in rejection or even betrayal, when there is no one else around with energy to match.

The literature of therapy talks about the method of choice for dealing with passive people. Challenge them, but not in the cerebral, distant, and Olympian manner of the Synthesist. Challenge them realistically. Tap into their potential energy in terms of the here-and-now situation. That is where Realists excel.

When Practical Solutions Are Needed—Now

Margo was in a small fishing boat, on a holiday with friends, three miles off the Kenya coast in the Indian Ocean. Suddenly the engine died, and then, for mysterious reasons, the boat began to sink. Before they knew what was happening, Margo, her three friends, and the African boatman were in the sea. They all had life jackets, but it was a long way to shore. Around them were floating a number of wooden hatch covers and a spar or two. Suddenly one of the men announced that he didn't know how to swim.

Margo took charge. She barked orders. She told each person to take a hatch cover and, using it as a float, to begin kicking slowly toward shore. She ordered the non-swimmer to share a spar with her. Kick softly, she told him—don't stir up the water more than you have to.

With Margo's firm, no-nonsense presence next to him, the non-swimmer avoided panic. When he clumsily began to kick noisily every now and then, Margo ordered him to stop. Slowly and quietly, the five moved toward the distant shore.

Two hours later they all reached the beach, exhausted but safe. Tiredly, the non-swimmer asked Margo why she had been so insistent about going slowly and quietly, not splashing.

"Because," she said, "for one thing I knew it was a long way and we had to conserve our energy. For another, that ocean is full of sharks and I didn't care to attract their attention. And if I'd told you that, you might have panicked and none of us would have made it."

Margo's story may be a trifle more dramatic than the situations in which most of us are likely to find ourselves. But it typifies another strength of the Realist—when the going gets tight, and there is a need for hard, practical solutions and for someone to take charge, the Realist excels.

"We Need to Move on This"

The Israeli Army owes a great deal of its success to its unique organizational structure and its philosophy of leadership. Contrary to the practice of virtually every other military organization ever known, the army of Israel is almost without hierarchy. Differences in rank and methods for reporting through channels are established for purely administrative purposes. When it comes to field training and to actual combat, it is an army of peers, in which every soldier (male or female) is in effect a commander, expected to make immediate decisions.

The Israeli Army's greatest virtue is its ability to move quickly and imaginatively, to respond to attack from any number of directions at once. Much of that capability stems from the philosophy of "every soldier a commander." War, to the Israelis, is a matter of immediacy, flexibility, and realism, rather than of detailed analysis or comprehensive planning. The Israelis are responsive and reactive, and that demands an empirical approach—a focus on the facts at hand and the here-and-now—on the part of every soldier.

Under some circumstances we can't afford analysis, speculation, experiment, or a focus on the long range and all the possible alternatives. We need the immediate, concrete approach of the Realist.

Realists are at their best, then, in situations where there is a need for energy in organizing, for immediate practical solutions, and for decisive movement. One of the virtues of Realists is their instinctive ability to recognize such situations when they occur. And seldom do they hang back. They may not recognize the title "catalyst" as theirs, but it is.

The Importance of Situational Self-Knowledge

Let us summarize what can be learned from this chapter.

Each Style of Thinking contains strengths that excel in certain situations. Those strengths need to be acknowledged, understood, developed, and used purposefully. We need to know how to recognize those situations that call for the application of our preferred strategies. Confronted with those situations, we need to use our strengths confidently.

Here we will list, in a short table, each Style of Thinking and the general sort of situation in which it is likely to be most effective:

Style of Thinking	General Situation
Synthesist	The Mind-Boggling Mess
Idealist	The Care and Nurturing of Quality
Pragmatist	"Where Do We Go from Here?"
Analyst	Negotiating the Straight and Narrow
Realist	Getting the Show on the Road

And here are our recommendations for how to go about making the most productive use of your strengths:

1. Understand your preferred Style or Styles of Thinking, how they work and the strategies that are typical of them.

2. Understand what your Styles of Thinking are good for. Learn to acknowledge and respect your strengths, rather than wishing you were different.

3. Pick your best situations; that is, learn what they are likely to be and how to recognize them.

4. Use your strengths purposefully, when the situation calls for them.

5. Accept and enjoy your just rewards when your efforts are successful.

In this chapter we have looked at the inherent strengths of each of the Styles of Thinking, and have reiterated how those strengths are at their most productive in appropriate situations. But what about situations in which your preferred strategies are not so appropriate, where other strategies are called for?

To deal with that issue, we come to the question of skill development, learning the skills and strategies of other Styles of Thinking. That is the subject of the next chapter.

Chapter XI

EXTENDING AND AUGMENTING
YOUR THINKING STRATEGIES

George Lewis, a Pragmatist-Idealist, went to work for a new company. He soon discovered that the people in charge, therefore those who got ahead, tended to be people who valued structure and the "bottom line"—in other words, Analysts and Realists.

Wishing to rise in the company, George set himself a task—to learn how accountants and budget people do what they do. He realized that, more than simply learning new methods, he had to learn entirely new ways of thinking. So he patiently plodded through the mysteries of ledgers, financial statements, and budget procedures, fighting the impulse to skip ahead when the numbers began to run together. It was painful and unnatural for him, but it helped George immeasurably in his later years with the company.

Without knowing it, George did what anyone does who wants to extend and augment the set of thinking strategies learned and reinforced during one's growing-up years. He deliberately learned the strategies of Styles of Thinking which were not "natural" to him. He exposed himself to methods and techniques that to him seemed unnatural, uncomfortable, and even downright silly. He learned how they worked, he practiced them in low risk situations, and, in time, incorporated them into his mode of operation.

To accomplish this kind of learning does not require that you change your personality, or your value system, or your worldview. It *does* mean a change in behavior, one that is conscious, purposeful, and entirely within your control.

Three things make this new learning possible:

1. Knowing that you are likely to have "blind spots" in your thinking. Your lowest scores on the I_nQ are clues to those blind spots.

2. Understanding that the process of learning new skills will feel uncomfortable and unnatural. Those we have worked with in this learning process have invariably reported initial distaste in carrying out the tasks needed to learn low preference Styles of Thinking.

3. Knowing in a very specific way what you are trying to learn, and which activities promote that learning. Here, we believe, is the greatest benefit that can come from a focus on cognitive style rather than personality, managerial style, or even interpersonal style.

In this chapter, we shall take each Style of Thinking in turn, and offer suggestions for increasing your proficiency in using the strategies of each Style.

But before you rush to practice these activities and exercises, give some thought to these questions:

—Given what you know now about the five Styles of Thinking, and your scores on the I_nQ, in which do you see that your skills are relatively underused or underdeveloped?

—Given your personal goals and needs, in which of the five Styles of Thinking can augmentation benefit your career, profession, personal life, or relations with others?

—To what extent are you willing to put up with the trouble and discomfort involved in learning new ways of thinking?

A further caution: Some of the suggested activities are going to sound strange, weird, sometimes outrageous. It is precisely those to which you will find it valuable to pay the most attention.

Improving Your Synthesist Skills

☐ Practice listening for conflict and disagreement.
This is a good exercise for Idealists, who aren't used to thinking

about listening in such a way. Idealists are adept at tuning out any undertones or overtones in social discourse that sound at all "negative."

Listen behind the humor and politeness. Listen, for a change, to what *isn't* being said. Instead of ignoring the tension in a conversation, pay attention to it. Try to understand the disagreement that isn't quite being expressed, and how it might affect the outcome of the discussion or conversation.

In your own conversations with others, when you find yourself feeling tension in the face of real or imagined disagreement, confront the tension and ask yourself what it might mean. To what extent are you or the other person feeling threatened? Why?

Once you start to listen in this way, you may be amazed at how much basic information you have been in the habit of overlooking.

☐ Ask dumb–smart questions.

"All right," you say to your staff, "I understand that you want to reorganize the typing pool so that everyone shares a particular secretary. That may be a good way to go. But what happens if, in a particular situation, one person gives the secretary twice as much work as the other person does?"

At first you may get this reaction: "Well, if you're so smart, what do you think?" Or more subtly: "That means you don't like the idea, you negative jerk!"

But stick with it. Make it clear that you expect others to bolster their bright ideas and recommendations with thoughtful attention to anticipating and countering potential negative effects. When they see the point and do it, praise them.

The strategy is also a good means for developing clear thinking and responsibility in children. It is a positive use of devil's advocacy.

☐ Develop the third-party observer viewpoint.

It is relatively easy to find opportunities to practice the third-party skill. The next time you attend a meeting, when you don't have to be in charge, try acting as a third-party observer.

Sit back and watch the action. Listen to what people say, but more importantly, listen to the *way* they say it. Watch how people interact with one another, how they try to influence each other. Draw a diagram showing who speaks to whom and how often. Try to understand the shifting of power in the group. Watch nonverbal communications, and make guesses about what they mean.

Deliberately shift your focus. Pay less attention than you normally would to the substance of the discussion (what it's about) and more to the process (what happens and how it happens). Try not to judge what people say, not to take sides, and not to get personally involved. In other words, give your ego a holiday during the meeting. Work at simply describing what's going on.

Then begin to study your own part in the process. See if you can be just as descriptive of your own role in the learning stage, and later, when you are once again active as a participant.

When you have learned to use this skill, you will find yourself being able to move from actor to observer and back again, on your own volition. The accomplished third-party observer is both observer and participant at the same time, and conscious of both at all times.

You may never attain that level of perceptual flexibility but stick with it. See how the exercise broadens your perception of people and their odd and varied ways.

☐ Look for relationships between things that have no apparent likeness.

Arthur Koestler once described the creative process as one of *bisociation,* which means precisely this: combining two unlike things to make something new and surprising. That is a Synthesist procedure.

For example, is there a connection between a manager's technical expertness and the degree to which he or she delegates work? The answer is Yes—how many reasons can you find for the relationship?

Try a study of your own, one having to do with design, perhaps, or the intuitive look of things. What might the relationship be, for instance, between patterns of bird migration and the record of prehistoric Indian settlements in America?

☐ Practice improving your tolerance for eccentricity.

For starters, watch "Monty Python's Flying Circus," especially if you can't stand it.

Read Kurt Vonnegut, S. J. Perelman, and Lewis Carroll.

Take a course in Synectics if you have the opportunity.

If your local university extension has a course in improvisatory theater or modern dance, take it. Let your hair down.

Go into an art museum. Find the craziest, most "far-out" abstract paintings possible. Stand there and stare at them. Don't read the titles or try to figure out what they "are." Just gaze as long as you can, letting the colors and patterns flow over and around you. Do that as long as you can stand it. Next week, go back and try to double your tolerance time. Treat the process like jogging or swimming laps in a pool.

☐ When someone seems to come out of left field, stop and listen carefully.

A number of fruitful studies of schizophrenia have shown that even the maunderings of the mentally ill have their peculiar kind of relevance. The relevance may be through analogy and the meaning may be intensely personal, but there is a connection that makes sense when understood.

In other words, one person's non sequitur is the next person's crystalline logic.

If you can, find an opportunity to eavesdrop on a group of four-year-old children, chattering as they play. You will be listening to the intelligence of the human mind before it has been chained and fettered by logic. Perhaps that is what we hear in the occasionally "off-the-wall" notions tossed out by Synthesists. To discover and understand such notions in others may be a way for you to rediscover a little of your own lost cognitive innocence.

☐ Practice negative analysis.

Try this exercise carefully the first few times. Adopt a musing, "What if" tone and keep a smile on your face. Don't be too serious about it.

Let's say your club has enthusiastically rallied around the idea of sponsoring a charity ball. The plan is to issue two thousand invitations and hope for five hundred attendees at so much per couple. Try asking, in a whimsical way, "What happens if we don't break even?" There is likely to be a chorus of, "Oh, but we will!"

Or be helpful by quickly running through all the action steps involved in planning. When a possible negative effect pops up, raise an eyebrow and say, "I suppose it's possible that more than five hundred people will show up." Wait for someone else to say, "But the hall only holds five hundred!"

Improving Your Idealist Skills

☐ Focus on the whole, not the "one best way."

Assume you are a member of a group that has the task of planning a new community center, say as an outgrowth of your church. Instead of plotting a linear path to your goal at the beginning, try this:

Give each member of the group a number (say three or five) of blank 5 by 8 inch index cards, and a wide-tipped felt marking pen. Give the group these instructions:

> "In order to get our project going and completed, there are any number of things that have to be done, any number of specific steps. On each of your cards, print an idea. That idea represents an action step that you feel has to be done. You have five cards, so list the five most important steps that you see as necessary."

Once all the cards have been completed, have people take pieces of tape and post the cards on the wall, randomly. Then clump them into areas of duplication and similarity. You will quickly have assembled a dramatic, visual picture that everyone can see of people's opinions about priorities and alternatives.

Have people sort the cards into a sequence of action steps— what has to be done first, second, and on down the line. The group may even add more steps that hadn't been thought of on the first round. The group will eventually come up with a more or less linear plan that shows just how and in what order the project will be completed.

Using an approach like this, you come out with something like a "one best way" Analyst product, but you have gotten there by using an assimilative, Idealist technique that brings to light all the numerous possible alternatives, gives everyone a chance to participate in planning, and helps to get them to agree on both the goal and the way to get there.

☐ Focus on the long range.

You are forty years old, and you've become tired of working for someone else. You have saved up a respectable amount of money to invest, and a franchise in Yummy-Burgers is available two blocks from your home. You could be your own boss if you were to buy the franchise. You could walk to work every day. Your Realist immediately says, "Let's go!" Your Pragmatist restlessness and opportunism tell you it's the thing to do.

Hold it!

Write a long-range scenario. Ask what things will be like five years from now if you were to make the move. Don't limit yourself to money. Think broadly and assimilatively. Think about your family, your social status, the effect on your time and freedom, everything you can think of that might be part of that future. Do a thorough, conscientious job of it. Then decide.

☐ Think about high standards and superordinate goals.

You are sales manager in a manufacturing firm. You are used to thinking about results, achievement, the "bottom line." The only reports you care about are monthly sales summaries and prospect lists.

At an executive staff meeting you hear the personnel manager say, "One of the most pressing needs we have is to build career paths for the women in this company. Our future depends on it, it seems to me, as well as the overall productivity of the firm."

Your first impulse is to say something like, "How do you translate that into sales dollars and market share?"

Try instead to pose a different question. "Can you expand on that? Why would that be a good thing to do?"

Then listen. The personnel manager may have some ideas you hadn't thought of. See if you can share in his odd vision of the world.

☐ Listen for value statements and aspirations.

This can be a particularly difficult exercise for Realists. Therefore, the exercise is to be commended to them.

If you are a Realist and you believe that your spouse has a good deal of the Idealist quality, pay particular attention to this exercise. It may enrich your marriage, because that look of frustrated helplessness you begin to see was there all the time. You were so busy solving immediate problems you overlooked it.

Listen for emotional undertones and overtones. Suspend your judgment when the other person seems to be irrationally sentimental or idealistic. Treat your spouse's aspirations as if they were just as real as the facts that you see before you.

If you work hard at this kind of listening, your spouse may be eternally grateful. Certainly he or she will be surprised.

Be prepared for some shocking differences in perception that may emerge from an exercise like this one. Proceed with care, and caring.

☐ Try to fit a number of differing ideas under a common framework.

Laurence Tribe, Professor of Law at Harvard and an acute thinker on social policy, calls this process "groping upward." It means a conscious effort to reconcile disagreement by having the conflicting parties search for the Idealist "umbrella" that can accommodate all views. Here is an example:

> You have built a home on your desert property near Tucson. You moved there because you love the peace and quiet of the desert. Just down the road someone has built a new house, and you discover to your horror that your new neighbors own several motorcycles. You hate motorcycles because of their noise and the damage that you are afraid they may do to the fragile desert environment.
>
> You become acquainted with your new neighbor, and you make an interesting discovery. You both came to this area because of a love for the tranquillity of the desert. It happens that you enjoy it in different ways. You like to just sit on your patio and listen to the silence. He and his family like to ride their motorcycles out into the backcountry and do much the same thing.

You carefully express to your neighbor your fears about the noise and damage of motorcycles, and you find that he agrees in principle. He is as concerned as you are about uncontrolled riding in the area. Together you sponsor a resolution to the county board of supervisors that leads to an ordinance restricting motorcycles to main roads and certain designated backcountry areas of the county. As time goes on, you join in enforcing the ordinance.

You and your neighbor, in this example, have "groped upward" to a common goal and a common understanding. Purposeful use of an Idealist strategy has taken you beyond a very real conflict at the immediate surface level, where Realists, Analysts, and even Pragmatists often prefer to stand and fight.

☐ Encourage others to express their aspirations.

Earlier we talked about listening for value statements and aspirations, in order to learn to tolerate them. Here we suggest you go a step further.

Aspirations are things that Analysts and Realists tend to overlook. Aspirations aren't the same as concrete results or the logical outcome of plans. They are usually vague, abstract images of the future.

Try this approach with your children. Instead of the usual, "What do you want to be when you grow up?" ask, "How would you like things to be in your life?"

Then listen, and don't judge.

The exercise can be especially useful to a manager or supervisor. Encouraging the expression of aspirations, in a nonjudgmental way, can increase the involvement of others in planning and decision making. Just as importantly, knowing something about others' aspirations gives you valuable information about your leadership environment, namely, what is going on inside your people. You can open up a whole new dimension of "facts," intangible and abstract as they may seem.

Improving Your Pragmatist Skills

☐ Practice thinking incrementally.

Millie was a young teacher and aspiring writer, who
wanted to travel and see the world. She thought that being a
travel writer would be an ideal career.

She learned how to write snappy query letters, and began
making contacts with magazines. As a teacher, she contacted
every international agency she could think of, letting them
know of her talents and availability. She got very little response from those efforts.

Entirely by chance, during a luncheon conversation, Millie
learned of a short-term teaching opportunity that was open in
a Latin American country. The place wasn't high on the list
of countries where she wanted to go, but she seized the
chance. As a result of that trip, she was able to write and sell
travel articles on the country to two magazines.

Millie was on her way, with overseas experience in teaching
and published articles in her résumé. She suddenly found
doors open to her, but not as a result of careful planning and
goal-setting; simply by being alert and taking advantage of
opportunities.

Incremental thinking is reactive, adaptive thinking. Its utility
depends on your willingness to stop agonizing over achieving the
ideal or the complete, and settling for the immediate, using opportunities as stepping-stones to get where you want to go.

☐ Allow others to experiment, and try to join in.

Lydia says she wants to try a new filing system? So long as it
won't disrupt the whole office, let her try it out. Monitor the results with her, and reward her if it works. Even if it doesn't, reward her for trying.

George has in mind a new sales approach? Give him permission, and pay attention to how it goes, even though you know privately that "we tried that once and it didn't work."

Most mistakes are not fatal, but all mistakes can be opportunities for learning. Pragmatists know that in their bones—the rest of us have to work at it. Give others the chance to experiment and learn through error. And give yourself the same opportunity.

☐ Look for the short-range payoff.

> YOU: Our immediate need is to be visible to the public. We should have a brochure that we can distribute everywhere it's likely to get attention.
>
> THEY: But we have to be sure of what it says about us. We don't want to look careless or phony. It's important that we say just the right things. We'll have to work very carefully on that.
>
> YOU: Then let's compromise. We'll hire a professional copywriter, and give him or her the basic information and a deadline. It may not be exactly what we want, but we'll be able to get it out quickly. Meanwhile you guys can start working on a real quality product.

When the need for a short-run payoff is clear, don't hesitate. Of course that means *if* you can afford it, but sometimes you can't afford anything else.

☐ Learn to think tactically.

> Bob used to be an undercover agent in the military. His job was to figure out how to get through the security systems of top secret installations. His objective was to keep the commanders of those installations on their toes, and involved in continually improving their security.
>
> Bob got so good at his job that he reached a point where there was no security system that he couldn't penetrate. Sometimes it took a month, sometimes as long as a year, but he never failed in the long run.
>
> When he first started, Bob used to assume that everyone thought much the same way as he did. He became successful when he understood how to begin putting himself in the place of people who thought in ways entirely different from

his own. His security penetration was always based on figuring out the habits, patterns, and peculiarities of the people who were supposed to be responsible for stopping him.

Bob would devise a set of tactics for breaking through, and then he would test it by pretending he was the person on the other side. The key was his understanding that the other person wasn't like him, but someone very different. He would, in effect, rehearse and "role play" his adversary's countertactics.

If you are planning a political campaign, thinking of some community action plan, wanting a promotion, or trying to get some new project going in your company, you can't afford not to practice tactical thinking.

The thing to remember is, no matter how noble your cause may be, there is always someone or some force standing in the way of it. Good intentions, laudable aims, and a detailed plan will carry you only so far. Tactics and shrewdness are essential to success.

Ask these questions:

1. Who is on my side? What forces are in my favor? What other forces and people are potential support? How do I get them on my side?

2. Who may be against me? What forces are operating in opposition to me? Why?

3. What can I do to minimize those opposing forces? What are my options? How are those opposing forces likely to react to each of my options?

Once you start thinking this way, you are learning to think tactically. Never assume that your opponents think the way you do. There are always opponents, even to Utopia.

☐ Practice being "marketing."

Remember the case of Richard Noonan, the financial expert in Chapter V who was going to advise small colleges on their investment programs. And how they wouldn't buy his ideas.

Suppose Noonan had carefully, collaboratively offered his skills as an investment manager, and had proposed that his clients allow him to channel only 5 or 10 percent of their investment assets into high-yield programs, then to check the results. With such short-term objectives and small commitment, they might have bought the idea. Then he could have accelerated his activity, once having proved its worth to cautious, idealistic clients. We suspect he may have survived that way.

Being marketing is simply thinking in terms of what will sell and what people will buy. Very often, it is the opposite of the "all or nothing" approach. If you can't sell your whole package, you can usually sell a part of it. The key is knowing your customer, and treating that person as a special, unique market.

☐ Try being less tediously serious and more playful, especially with ideas and plans.

If this is difficult for you, try some basic loosening-up exercises first:

Play charades with friends.

Spend some time trying to write poetry, the more free-form the better.

Be a rambunctious horsie to your grandchildren, nephews, or nieces, if you have them. Really let go, make horsie noises, think like a horsie.

Make up nonsensical lyrics to a song and sing them out loud.

Try having fun in bed.

Once you have done some of these things, and discovered that lightning didn't strike you down after all, you are ready to be playful in a more serious vein.

Do you occasionally have an absurd or ridiculous idea in the midst of a serious meeting? Next time you have one, think about it, rephrase it to minimize the shock on all the sobersides in the crowd, and try it out. You may be surprised when your playful idea turns out to be the most useful thing anyone has suggested all day.

Improving Your Analyst Skills

☐ Study statistics or operations research.

We haven't the space to give a short course here, but look into these fields. What you can learn from them is the Analyst satisfaction of ordering and controlling data, of structuring problems, so as to make them easier to solve.

Don't fool yourself into thinking that a kind of analytical magic will come to you. Statistical methods always rest on value judgments, estimates, assumptions, and guesswork. But you can learn some of the discipline. At the very least, you can begin to understand the language of professional researchers, systems analysts, and other experts, who previously may have seemed to be speaking in a foreign tongue.

☐ Learn to gather more data before a decision.

Start with something simple, such as planning a trip. Or the need for a new car. List all the options, and compare them carefully and rigorously against standard choice criteria—that is, things you need and would like to have.

If you have an Analyst boss, and you are asked to make a recommendation on an important decision, delay it until you have gathered as much relevant information as you find practical and have time to amass. Chances are your boss will be tickled pink if you have, for once, actually performed an *analysis*. And if you are not very good at it the first time, your boss will probably be happy to help you learn, realizing that there is some hope for you after all.

☐ Learn to make a flowchart.

A flowchart is simply an accurate display, step by step, of the details of a task or a process. Try to make one for your work, your office, or some basic activity that you engage in. If you do a thorough job you may discover just how much wasted motion and energy go into your basic activities.

People in the human services area—counselors, social workers, health professionals—tend to have heavy Idealist loadings, and they often reject the use of such strongly analytical tools. They express a fear that such tools may "mechanize" or "dehumanize" their work. Yet it is exactly the kind of discipline which could help them use their skills and their all-too-limited resources more effectively and efficiently.

☐ Learn to tolerate quantification.

Suppose you were to use a quantified approach in a situation where people were being evaluated, such as comparing candidates for a job or a promotion, or comparing a number of patients in a clinic to decide who should receive the most services. Suppose you decided to assign numbered weights to your selection criteria, and also to the people involved, in terms of the extent to which each person meets each criterion.

Idealists often complain that such techniques are "inhuman." "You can't put people in boxes and then put numbers on them," they say. Synthesists might say, "That kind of system is artificial. There's too much petty detail." Both Pragmatists and Realists are apt to object, "It's too complicated. It takes too much time."

There is some truth in each of those opinions. Yet such methods can be useful in structuring and sorting out complex problems. Recognize that the numbers are only "proxy measures." They are not real, but they are useful indicators. They can be an effective means of objectifying prejudices and removing the bias of preconceived opinions.

☐ Pay greater attention to detail.

Proofread everything you write—carefully. Especially, learn to double-check any calculations you make, no matter how boring the task is.

Are you one who does things quickly, intuitively, incrementally, experimentally, and sloppily? If so, the first thing you are likely to notice, when you undertake to learn Analyst skills, is how quickly you get bored and lose concentration.

Learning the basic Analyst skill of paying attention to detail is the not-so-simple task of enforcing self-discipline. If you often send out letters that are "dictated, but not read" (rather a slipshod if not insulting practice, when you think about it), try *not* to do it for a month or two. You may find, after a while, that you feel a steadiness and solidity, knowing that your letters have been perfect in every detail, that they not only say exactly what you want to say, but that they reflect your confidence that you know what you're doing.

People who are poor proofreaders and double-checkers tend to be fast readers, who see whole phrases if not paragraphs, whole

sheets of figures and designs rather than the components. The Analyst approach requires that you focus on every word, every number, one at a time. When people begin to do that, they are often
shocked at just how sloppily they put their work together.

☐ Focus on constraints.

This is a particularly useful exercise for Idealists and Pragmatists, both of whom, in their different ways, would prefer to assume that good intentions and experimental energy are sufficient
to get things done.

Ask such questions as:

1. What is the deadline for completing the project?
2. What exactly are the available resources (people, equipment, money)?
3. Are the resources really sufficient for getting the project
done on time?
4. What are the probable barriers standing in the way of
doing the job properly?

And so forth.

The discipline amounts to substituting analytical objectivity for
rosy expectations, hopefulness, and faith.

Improving Your Realist Skills

☐ Focus on concrete results.

Jack says: "I'm tired of these big utility bills. Let's build a
greenhouse."

His wife Julia says: "Why a greenhouse? And where?"

"To take advantage of the sunshine in winter," Jack says.
"We'll become completely independent of the utility company, absolutely self-sufficient. We can put it out around the
front porch, facing south."

"Which way does the porch face?"

"Oh. Southwest," Jack responds. "I guess we'll have to
build it on an angle."

Julia, a Realist, says, "I'd like to see what it looks like before we go ahead with it."

So Jack draws up a plan, and he and Julia look it over.

"It looks odd, doesn't it?" Julia says.

"Yeah, it does. Sort of like a sail blowing loose in the wind."

"And very complicated to build, with all those angles."

"Yes," Jack agrees. "Hm . . ."

"What about the neighborhood?"

Jack sighs. "It's too different, I'm afraid. The neighbors would object, and the value of our house would probably sink out of sight."

"Then let's find another way," Julia says.

The Realist skill of being concrete about a result can save a good deal of time, money, frustration, and disappointment.

☐ Focus on resources.

Let's return to Jack and Julia, and assume they are intent on building the greenhouse after all. They list the resources they'll need:

> Money: If they build it, the materials for the greenhouse will cost about six hundred dollars. If they have it built, it will cost at least three thousand dollars. Things are tight right now—they can only swing about five hundred.
>
> Skills: Jack has never built anything more complicated than a bookcase. Julia has never built anything in her life. They will have to learn from scratch, which will mean more time and probably more money because of inevitable mistakes.
>
> Time: Both of them have to work full time. They would have only weekends to spare for the construction, probably for two or three months, and no time for anything else.

Resource questions are a specialty of Realists, and easy to learn. The problem is to be *truly* Realist about the answers—that is, honest and tough-minded, looking at the problem straight on—which often means being pessimistic rather than relying on optimism.

☐ Practice getting to the point quickly.

This exercise is intended for Analyst-Idealists. Often they have a hard time believing that anyone could accept a report or an explanation unless every nook and cranny, every tack and pin, every value and need has been thoroughly documented and verbalized. It may feel at first like biting your tongue, but try it the other way.

☐ Practice writing short, declarative sentences.

Such as the one above.

☐ Learn to paraphrase for precision.

Here is a useful exercise for two people who both suffer from discursiveness, long-windedness, prolixity, and the anxiety of believing they won't be understood unless everything is spilled out and spelled out.

First, agree that you both want to learn to be succinct. Then, choose a subject for discussion. Person A starts out, say, by explaining "the current crisis in South Africa," in his or her usual interminable style. Person B listens and times the explanation with a stopwatch. Person B then paraphrases the explanation as succinctly as possible, while Person A runs the stopwatch. Continue through two or three reiterations, back and forth, with the aim of cutting the time in half each time. Then start over and rotate the order on a new subject.

You may be amazed at how much easier it is to understand each other without most of those words you used to think were absolutely essential.

☐ Practice incisiveness.

Next time you find yourself enjoying a theoretical, analytical, or conceptual discussion, stop and ask, "What are the practical applications?"

Now, we are not trying to rob Synthesists and Analysts of their fun. We are merely suggesting that they might want to try the exercise, in order to learn this valuable Realist skill.

Bone up on Quantum Mechanics, for instance. Theorize and speculate at each other until you've had enough, then raise the question of practical applications. Search for them, and get as specific as possible. Keep at it until you are sure that a Realist would be satisfied. Try out your routine on a Realist. Then go back and practice some more.

A *Summing Up*

Let's assume that you have tried some of these tasks, that you have really applied yourself to learning the strange strategies of another Style of Thinking. How will you feel, and how well will you do in real life?

At first, you will feel awkward. For a while, you may not do at all well.

We have observed many people who have gone through the learning process. Here is what we have concluded:

Learning the strategies of a new Style of Thinking is like learning to speak a foreign language. If you work hard, you learn verbs, grammar, vocabulary, and all the rest of the technicalities. But fluency is always another matter, as all serious students of language know. At first you make mistakes, you feel hesitant and unnatural. Fluency comes with practice, with using what you know, talking with and listening to others who are fluent. It requires that you take the risk of being wrong and feeling silly when you say something wrong. But that is precisely what it takes to learn.

Good luck in your learning.

Chapter XII

THEORY FOR THOSE WHO WANT THEORY

In this chapter we propose to touch upon some of the theory and research which provide a foundation for this book.

There are certainly important theoretical questions relevant to Styles of Thinking. What are the connections between how people think and their behavior? Are Style of Thinking preferences fixed, or can they be changed? How do differences in Styles of Thinking develop? We hope and expect that these and similar questions will be dealt with in future research by ourselves and others.

However, it is not our intention here to present and justify a theory of Styles of Thinking.[1] Our area of practice is applied and practical. Our own research has been directed at measuring differences in Style of Thinking preferences and, in a structured and consistent way, observing the effects of those preferences in everyday life. Some of the findings from that research have been reported in the preceding chapters.

What initially captured our interest in developing the I_nQ was the fact that several different lines of research, carried out by both experimental and applied scientists of varying conceptual persuasions, had arrived at roughly the same formulation: that people do indeed think differently. That this formulation helped us make immediate sense of what we saw our clients, friends, and selves

---

[1] We will use the term Styles of Thinking Theory throughout this chapter. We do it for convenience, but in no way do we assert that our formulations have reached the status of a theory. Rather, they are ordered statements which need much further testing and development.

doing every day was the deciding factor in determining our own decision to move ahead.

Here, then, in necessarily brief form, are some of the conceptual bases that underlie our work, and that have provided much of the stimuli for it. For those who wish to read further, we have listed, at the end of the book, some studies that we believe will provide the best start. See Reading List which follows.

Motivated Strategies

Very little that human beings do is done randomly or without reason. When an infant reaches out, he or she does not reach out randomly for long, because reaching out results in something happening. A shiny rattle, the bar of the crib, a parent's face or hand are touched and felt, and that touching feels either good or bad. In this way the child learns about the world, not only as "that stuff out there which isn't me," but also as a place which is sometimes gratifying and sometimes not.

As Johnny and Jenny grow, they acquire more and more knowledge of what does and what doesn't work for them in getting the most satisfaction and the least frustration. At first their satisfactions are basic and general: relief of discomfort, food, warmth, a tender presence. Later rewards become more and more tangible and specific: a particular food, relief of pain to a specific part of the body, a loving touch from a special person.

In the same way, initially, "knowledge" is vague and the learning process is simple and mechanistic. But, in time, the miracle of thinking begins. The child gains conscious and direct awareness of what it wants and some ideas about how to get it.

That awareness has two principal parts. First, a kind of mapping of the immediate world: what's out there and what it does. Most psychologists agree that the initial maps are full of distortions. The world from the perspective of the playpen is full of magical surprises and an assortment of optical illusions. But distorted or not, that picture can provide a basis for action. This it must do if the child is to get along in the world.[2]

[2] There is some disagreement among developmental psychologists about how much of the uncanny ability of children to make sense of the world is a part of our human inheritance, and how much is the result of learning.

Simply having impressions of what the world is like doesn't help Johnny get what he wants from it. To do that he has to do something, to take some action in a purposive way. Some of those actions will succeed and be reinforced. Others will make things worse, or simply not work, and they will be dropped. Thus, in time, as his world becomes differentiated, and as wants and don't-wants are identified, the child begins to acquire a repertoire of strategies.

The specific activities and ways of thinking that make up these strategies evolve out of the complex set of circumstances in which Johnny and Jenny grow up. Given an inborn temperament, a particular set of talents, parental and sibling examples, models and crazinesses, a whole host of outside reality factors, and a unique set of wants and needs, each of us ends up with our own quite different set of strategies.

Those strategies, continually refined and embellished, carry over through adolescence and eventually into adulthood as basic modes of operating. We believe that preferences in Styles of Thinking develop precisely in this way.

Suppose that, as a small child, I am given to fantasy and the asking of unlikely questions. "Daddy, the moon looks like a face. Is there a man up there?" Daddy, a serious fellow, is in the habit of saying, "Don't be silly!" to such questions. After the nth time this has happened, and unless later influences strongly intervene, I am likely to reject fantasy and analogy as appropriate strategies for gaining knowledge. I may instead decide to be orderly and sensible in my inquiries, because that is how I saw Daddy proceed.

As I grow, I discover that there are certain ways of behaving that are considered proper, that are "shoulds." My mother, for instance, disapproves strongly when I appear selfish. "You should share your toys with your sister," she says. "You must always help smaller children when they are in trouble." "It's not nice to play roughly." "Jenny is always polite to grown-ups. You should be that way too." And not only does she say these things but I see her act them out in her own life. I grow up with certain values about sharing, helpfulness, gentleness, and the observation of adult proprieties. There is evidence that by the age of two, some children have already acquired such an altruistic way of looking at the world.

Similarly, Johnny grows up in an atmosphere of tension, anxious concern on the part of his parents for his health and welfare, and an ambience of careful procedure and control. From the start, he will develop strategies that are congruent with the atmosphere. They will be characterized by caution, careful testing, thorough evaluation of alternatives—in other words, an analytical approach to reality.

However, it is not at all certain that this will happen. For reasons now unclear (though the subject of much speculation), Johnny may show a strong need to control others and to be independent and free. In that case, as his wants interact with his reality, Johnny may become boldly assertive, carelessly taking risks. To the extent that this behavior and the thinking that prompts it work, they will become part of him.

Liability as Overuse of Strength

In *Man for Himself*, Erich Fromm suggested that important life strategies are learned to meet crucial problems of living. These strategies and the behavior they produce, he said, could be judged productive or nonproductive, depending upon how appropriate they were to the situation. That the same behavior might be both a strength and a weakness is not a new notion. But the idea that it is the overuse of potentially constructive behavior that makes the difference has been very useful to us. For instance, we found that the concept of overuse of a strength as a potential liability was a powerful tool with which to analyze data we had gathered on the behavior of "difficult" people.

But the most important point is that it makes clear why it is so useless to wish that you or someone you're having problems with were different. For when you wish away your or their liabilities, you also wish away the corresponding strength.[3]

Inquiry Modes

The technical name for Styles of Thinking is Inquiry Modes. Inquiry Modes are basic sets of purposive methods for making

[3] For the explication of this relationship between strength and liability as it applies to work settings, we owe a debt to Stuart Atkins, Allan Katcher, and Elias Porter, Jr.

sense of the world. They are built on early acquired preferences, on learned values, and on worldviews—concepts about the world and the nature of reality.

C. West Churchman, whose work forms so much of the foundation for this book, identified Inquiry Modes as methodologies that could be ascribed historically to certain seminal thinkers and philosophers. Justus Buchler, a philosopher at Columbia University, quite independently identified five distinct philosophical methodologies in much the same way. He did not use our Style of Thinking titles, but the five "styles" Buchler identifies correlate with considerable (and surprising) accuracy with the Churchman typology. We can show these relationships graphically, as in the table that follows.

Style of Thinking	Churchman, Inquiry Mode ascribed to:	Central Idea or Philosophy	Buchler, Methodology ascribed to:	Central Idea or Philosophy
Synthesist	Hegel	Dialectic, Phenomenology	Whitehead	Process Philosophy
Idealist	Kant	Philosophical Idealism	S. T. Coleridge	Neoplatonic Transcendentalism
Pragmatist	E. A. Singer	Philosophical Pragmatism	Dewey	Pragmatism, Social Experiment
Analyst	Leibniz	Symbolic Logic	Descartes	Scientific Method
Realist	Locke	Empiricism	Bentham	Utilitarianism

If we were to array the identification of these five basic categories as they appeared chronologically in Western thought, we would discover that the Analyst Style has the greatest antiquity, beginning with the Enlightenment and the origin of Scientific Method. The Pragmatist approach is the "youngest," having its beginnings barely a hundred years ago. We would find that the Idealist origin is closely connected with the rise of modern democracy and ideas concerning the perfectibility of humankind. The Realist approach is associated with the beginnings of the Industrial Revolution and modern economics.

A number of things are tentatively explained by all this. The three most common Styles of Thinking, as we have found, are the Idealist, Analyst, and Realist. The first is intimately associated with accepted societal values in philosophy, government, and political community. The second reflects the foundations of Western intellectual method. The third is closely tied to thought and activity in economics and production, or what might be called the empirical foundations of our society.

Pragmatist methods, less common than the other three, are relatively new, and generally associated (through John Dewey, for example) with non-traditional, experimental, and "progressive" thinking and action.

And what of the least common, the Synthesist? Ian Mitroff makes an interesting observation that may provide an answer. The dialectical method, as we know, is the basis of Synthesist inquiry. Dr. Mitroff points out that the dialectic has seldom been taught in America. It has never been an accepted mode of inquiry in this country, compared to others, though it is more the norm in Europe. Would we, if we were to administer the I_nQ across the Atlantic, find many more Synthesists there than over here? We have not yet done cross-cultural studies, but we see that as a next step for ourselves or others.

What we do know is that, as Kenneth Keniston has pointed out, we have had almost four hundred years of training, education, and indoctrination in the Analyst mode, rather less in the others, but at least a century of each.[4] Such traditions in thinking become a part of culture, therefore a part of the values of society.

Substantive vs. Functional Rationality

Few questions have occupied scholars, thinkers, and philosophers more than the question of substantive vs. functional rationality. Certainly it is important in terms of some of the practical, day-to-day issues that face us as a society.

Max Weber, the great German sociologist, first defined the substantive-functional dichotomy. Put most simply, it says this: There are two basic kinds of rationality in the world, two basic kinds of thinking.

[4] Keniston, in *The Uncommitted* (New York: Dell-Laurel, 1970).

Substantive rationality is that which is based on personal knowledge of the world. It rests on intuition, value judgments, what is felt or known without outside authority, on ethical and moral criteria. Substantive rationality produces knowledge which "comes to" the individual without analysis. It is often called "classical" rationality after our debt to the Greeks, especially Socrates, Plato, and Aristotle. The notion is that certain things—such as prudence, political reason, and the qualities that make for the good life—are known to people through experience, requiring neither instruction by others nor a formal intellectual process in order to be comprehended.

Functional rationality has its origin in scientific method, mathematics, and economics. It produces knowledge through analytical and empirical processes—deliberate, planned, formal inquiry. In fact, functional rationality often goes by the name of "formal" rationality, which is a way of saying that it is not "natural," as substantive rationality is often considered to be. Functional rationality is thought to be formally learned.

If substantive rationality is the rationality of intuition, values, and ethical judgment, functional rationality is the rationality of formal logic, structured inquiry, and efficiency.

The substantive-functional debate is important because it lies at the heart of every sort of social issue. Conservation vs. production, art vs. science, effectiveness vs. efficiency, the organic vs. the bureaucratic, tradition vs. progress, the small town vs. the big city, even East vs. West and human liberty vs. autocracy—all are heavily infused with the tension of this dichotomy.

Yet we have thought for a long time that the lines may be too tightly drawn, and may indeed be artificial. Data gathered with the I_nQ and its associated theory offer new suggestive insights into the old controversy.

Let's look first at the surface level. The functional-substantive dichotomy is often called the "fact-value" dichotomy (another term that we owe to Max Weber). It seems clear that the Synthesist and Idealist styles are strongly oriented toward the "value" side of the dichotomy, or substantive rationality. The Analyst and Realist approaches are clearly more oriented toward "facts," or formal, functional rationality. The Pragmatist, contingent approach either bridges the gap between the two or perhaps ignores the question altogether.

So with the notion of Style of Thinking combinations. The Idealist-Analyst, Idealist-Realist, and Synthesist-Realist combinations typify people who think and live in both realms—the substantive and the functional. Perhaps this is the reason for the internal tension we have seen in such combinations. Received societal wisdom in our country puts great stress on formal logic, scientific method, and so forth; and most of our institutions make a claim for efficiency and related values. If that is so, then such people may experience, in the microcosm of self, the tension of the dichotomy in the outside world.

But the positive side is this: Substantive-functional Style of Thinking combinations are just as powerful and useful as any. Indeed, they should be *more* useful than others because they make use of both kinds of rationality. They should have greater inherent versatility.

Suggestive examples of the need abound in our organizational life. The helping professions, for instance, so often strongly oriented toward a substantive valuing of the world, badly need an infusion of logic and efficiency, in order to carry out their tasks effectively under the constraints of limited resources. Engineering organizations, confronted by an increasing concern for the substantive values of conservation, environmental protection, and quality of life, can no longer be exclusively informed by functional, quantitative criteria.

The most productive thinkers may simply be those who are capable of thinking well in all five dimensions, thus on both sides of the dichotomy. If this is true, then such substantive-functional controversies as the relative emphasis in school curricula of the humanities versus science are specious. They are debates pursued by those who feel the power of their own Style of Thinking and are thus misled into denying equal power to ways of thinking quite different from their own.

Left-Brain and Right-Brain Thinking

Those who have studied the human brain have long known that it has two hemispheres, and that each performs specific functions.[5]

The right side of the brain is thought to govern the motor functions of the left side of the body. It is also the side that performs "nonrational" mental functions, such as intuition, pattern recognition, nonverbal communication, playfulness, abstraction, and the like.

The left hemisphere of the brain controls the right side of the body, and the "rational" functions of logic, calculation, verbal articulation, structured observation, analysis, and so forth.

Recent evidence that expands our knowledge of these differences has come from work with brain-impaired patients. In sum, the evidence suggests that people who have had damage to the left side of the brain suffer losses of speech, writing ability, and the ability to perform logical calculation. They continue, however, to function normally in terms of "nonrational" activities. And the opposite is found to be true. Damage to the right side of the brain results in loss of the spatial sense, of nonverbal skills, of such qualities as humor, color sensitivity, and intuition.

This evidence has led to speculation that differences in hemisphere dominance produce differences in thinking and in the approach to problems. Although it is yet highly speculative, these notions do provide support for the reality of preferences in Styles of Thinking. We see these as possible relationships:

Left-brain dominant people operate as we might expect, as Analysts and Realists. Right-brain dominant people tend to use those strategies that we have called Idealist and Synthesist. Thus we would expect accountants and engineers to be strongly left-brain, poets and writers to be right-brain. While our occupational norm data are yet incomplete, these tendencies do indeed occur.

If it were found that the anatomy and physiology of the brain does indeed govern the Styles of Thinking that people have developed, would that mean that nothing could be done to alter them?

---

[5] In the brief exposition that follows, we have greatly oversimplified the findings. The brain is a highly adaptable organ.

It is of course a possibility, one that would explain the persistence of Style of Thinking preferences throughout life.[6] But we doubt that the governance of the physical brain is at all absolute.

There is entirely too much evidence in favor of the mutability of the human mind. We suspect that the brain is capable of altering its own capabilities. There are too many people we have seen who have learned to think out of the "other side" of their brains.

For now, we will wait, and watch with great interest to see those further new discoveries in neurology and their connection with Styles of Thinking theory.

Conceptualizing Strategies

In 1956, Jerome Bruner and his associates published A *Study of Thinking*. Like most scientists who had studied thinking, they turned their attention to cognition as a general human attribute: How do *human beings* (or other animals) gather data, categorize them, and use them to make sense of the world? Differences in individual approaches to thinking received little attention, with exceptions, of course, some of which we will mention later.

Basically, A *Study of Thinking* reported the results of a five-year study of the problem solving, perceptual categorizing, and the conceptualizing process. It also included descriptions of four "ideal conceptual strategies," each used in varying degrees by study subjects. When, in our own efforts to understand more about how individuals make decisions, we reread this important work, we were excited and encouraged, for two reasons.

First, we saw an immediate connection between Bruner's conceptual strategies and four of the five Inquiry Modes identified by Churchman. Second, this evidence from the psychological laboratory added to our confidence that individual preferences in Styles of Thinking (as we were then calling them) were real and could be measured.

Here are Bruner's four strategies and the i_nQ styles with which we believe they correlate:[7]

---

[6] This statement is a surmise. We have not yet done longitudinal testing, other than to measure the reliability of the i_nQ.

[7] Adapted from Jerome S. Bruner et al., A *Study of Thinking*, New York: John Wiley & Sons, 1956. They credit Robert V. Seymour with first seeing "the way in which conceptualizing behavior could be treated as a strategy problem."

Simultaneous Scanning	*Idealist*
Holding all relevant data in the mind at the same time, and testing all hypotheses against the mass of data.	
Successive Screening	*Realist and/or Pragmatist*
Testing a single hypothesis at a time, limiting the focus to only the data that will help test the hypothesis.	
Conservative Focusing	*Analyst*
Picking an example and altering one attribute of that example at a time until the correct solution is found.	
Focus Gambling	*Synthesist*
Picking an example and changing several attributes at a time until a solution appears.	

Cognitive Styles

Other pertinent attributes of individual preferences in cognitive style have been studied. For example, individuals differ in the degree to which they attend to specific features of a problem ("sharpeners") or to the problem as a whole ("levelers").[8] They also differ in the degree to which they give emphasis to the abstract aspects of life or to the concrete. Good evidence exists that these differences affect the way people evaluate the performance of others, the boldness with which they approach others, and the kinds of educational situations in which they can best learn.

In *The Psychology of Personal Constructs*, George Kelly presented a perspective on human behavior in which the way individuals thought about their world determined the way they felt about it and what they did in it and to it. We have found Kelly's book, published first in 1955, stimulating and supportive of our task.

Studies of individual differences in thinking have recently begun

[8] See, for example, George Klein, *Perception, Motives and Personality*, San Francisco: Jossey-Bass, 1970.

to be reported in such psychological literature with increasing frequency, a fact that we find heartening. For while it is of value to understand people in general, such understanding is not of much practical use. In our dealings with others, most of us don't seek to understand or influence people at large. It is Sam and Sally and ourselves that we care about and need to approach in the best possible way.

Isn't There More Than Thinking?

Human beings are complex, not simple. For example, they think but they also feel. The relationship of thinking and feeling is interactional and cyclical. The way I structure my world makes me feel about it in certain ways. The way I feel affects what I pay attention to and how I make sense of it.

It gets even more complicated when we recognize that as adults we are full of role messages—little lists of prescriptive statements that tell us how to be a nurse, or an engineer, or a son, daughter, husband, or wife. Most people try to behave the way their roles tell them to, contradictory as they may be.

Every situation we are in, the very realities of our lives act like a selective suction to pull from us behavior that is most appropriate to the situation. How then can we, in this book, have the temerity to categorize people at all, much less categorize them solely in terms of their Styles of Thinking?

We have two replies.

The first is an acknowledgment that each person *is* truly unique and never completely predictable. Our Style of Thinking characterizations only describe *prototypes* (or "ideal types"). No one is a total Analyst or a total Synthesist. Yet, Analyst thinking is a human characteristic and knowing how much one has of it makes it possible to predict a good deal about how he or she is going to think about things.[9]

Our second reply, and the note on which we wish to end this book, refers you back to our brief discussion of Motivated Strategies Theory.

[9] For those who are interested in an insightful discussion of the values and dangers of categorizing people, we suggest Walter Mischel's article, "On the Interface of Cognition and Personality: Beyond the Person-Situation Debate," in *The American Psychologist* (Vol. 34, September 1979), pp. 740–54.

While people are decidedly complex, they are not by any means haphazard. Their complicated arrangements of thoughts, feelings, and roles are just that—arrangements. They are systems of strategies and perspectives held together at the service of the motivations that drive and pull them. The more that any of us is like a prototype Realist, the more likely we are to have Realist motivations, Realist values, and a Realist outlook on life.

As a society, we chiefly value four of the five Styles of Thinking. To the extent that that is true, the potential thinking strategies that are available for us to learn are limited. In that sense, society has as much influence over how we learn to think as our natural parents and the early lives we lived.

inQ

PREFERENCES IN WAYS OF ASKING QUESTIONS AND MAKING DECISIONS

By Allen F. Harrison, M.P.A. & Robert M. Bramson, Ph.D.

DIRECTIONS

This questionnaire has no right or wrong answers. It is a tool which can help you identify your preferred modes of thinking, asking questions, and making decisions. To be of maximum value to you, it is important that you respond as accurately as possible in terms of the way you believe you actually behave, not as you think you should.

Each item in this questionnaire is made up of a statement followed by five possible endings. Indicate the order in which you believe each ending applies to you. In the blank box to the right of each ending, fill in the number 5, 4, 3, 2 or 1, indicating the degree to which an ending is most like you (5) or least like you (1). Do not use any number more than once for any group of five endings. Even if two or more endings seem equally like you, rank them anyway. Each ending must be ranked, 5, 4, 3, 2 or 1.

EXAMPLE

Please fill in this example:

WHEN I READ A NON FICTION BOOK, I AM MOST LIKELY
TO PAY ATTENTION TO:

1. The quality of the writing in the book .... ☐ 1
2. The main ideas in the book .... ☐ 4
3. The way the book is organized .... ☐ 3
4. The writer's logic and reasoning .... ☐ 2
5. The inferences to be made from the book .... ☐ 5

Once you are sure you understand the directions given above,
please turn the page and proceed.

BRAMSON, PARLETTE, HARRISON AND ASSOCIATES
Wells Fargo Building
2140 Shattuck Ave., Berkeley, CA 94704
(415) 548-0811

A. WHEN THERE IS CONFLICT BETWEEN PEOPLE OVER
    IDEAS, I TEND TO FAVOR THE SIDE THAT:
    1. Identifies and tries to bring out the conflict.
    2. Best expresses the values and ideals involved.
    3. Best reflects my personal opinions and experience.
    4. Approaches the situation with the most logic and consistency.
    5. Expresses the argument most forcefully and concisely.

B. WHEN I BEGIN WORK ON A GROUP PROJECT, WHAT IS
    MOST IMPORTANT TO ME IS:
    1. Understanding the purposes and value of the project.
    2. Discovering the goals and values of individuals in the group.
    3. Determining how we are to go about doing the project.
    4. Understanding how the project can be of benefit to the group.
    5. Getting the project organized and under way.

C. GENERALLY SPEAKING, I ABSORB NEW IDEAS BEST BY:
    1. Relating them to current or future activities.
    2. Applying them to concrete situations.
    3. Concentration and careful analysis.
    4. Understanding how they are similar to familiar ideas.
    5. Contrasting them to other ideas.

D. FOR ME, CHARTS AND GRAPHS IN A BOOK OR ARTICLE
    ARE USUALLY:
    1. More useful than the narrative, if they are accurate.
    2. Useful, if they clearly display the important facts.
    3. Useful, if supported and explained by the narrative.
    4. Useful, if they raise questions about the narrative.
    5. No more and no less useful than other material.

E. IF I WERE ASKED TO DO A RESEARCH PROJECT, I WOULD
    PROBABLY START BY:
    1. Trying to fit the project into a broad perspective.
    2. Deciding if I can do it alone or will need help.
    3. Speculating about what the possible outcomes might be.
    4. Determining whether or not the project should be done.
    5. Trying to formulate the problem as thoroughly as possible.

Please transfer your answers to the corresponding boxes on the last page of the
test.

F. IF I WERE TO GATHER INFORMATION FROM NEIGHBORS ABOUT A COMMUNITY CONCERN, I WOULD PREFER TO:

1. Meet with them individually and ask specific questions.   ☐

2. Hold an open meeting and ask them to air their views.   ☐

3. Interview them in small groups and ask general questions.   ☐

4. Meet informally with key people to get their ideas.   ☐

5. Ask them to bring me all the relevant information that they have.   ☐

G. I AM LIKELY TO BELIEVE THAT SOMETHING IS TRUE IF IT:

1. Has held up against opposition.   ☐

2. Fits with other things that I believe.   ☐

3. Has been shown to hold up in practice.   ☐

4. Makes sense logically and scientifically.   ☐

5. Can be personally verified by observable facts.   ☐

H. WHEN I READ A MAGAZINE ARTICLE IN MY LEISURE TIME, IT IS LIKELY TO BE ABOUT:

1. How someone resolved a personal or social problem.   ☐

2. A controversial social or political issue.   ☐

3. An account of scientific or historical research.   ☐

4. An interesting, humorous person or event.   ☐

5. A true account of someone's interesting experience.   ☐

I. WHEN I READ A REPORT AT WORK, I AM LIKELY TO PAY THE MOST ATTENTION TO:

1. The relation of the conclusions to my own experience.   ☐

2. Whether or not the recommendations can be accomplished.   ☐

3. The validity of the findings, backed up by data.   ☐

4. The writer's understanding of goals and objectives.   ☐

5. The inferences that are drawn from the data.   ☐

J. WHEN I HAVE A TASK TO DO, THE FIRST THING I WANT TO KNOW IS:

1. What the best method is for getting the task done.   ☐

2. Who wants the task done and when.   ☐

3. Why the task is worth doing.   ☐

4. What effect it may have on other tasks that have to be done.   ☐

5. What the immediate benefit is for doing the task.   ☐

Please transfer your answers to the corresponding boxes on the last page of the test.

K. I USUALLY LEARN THE MOST ABOUT HOW TO DO SOME-
    THING NEW BY:
    1. Understanding how it is related to other things I know.
    2. Starting in to practice it as soon as possible.
    3. Listening to differing views about how it is done.
    4. Having someone show me how to do it.
    5. Analyzing how to do it the best way.

L. IF I WERE TO BE TESTED OR EXAMINED, I WOULD
    PREFER:
    1. An objective, problem-oriented set of questions on the subject.
    2. A debate with others who are also being tested.
    3. An oral-visual presentation covering what I know.
    4. An informal report on how I have applied what I have learned.
    5. A written report covering background, theory, and method.

M. PEOPLE WHOSE ABILITIES I RESPECT THE MOST ARE
    LIKELY TO BE:
    1. Philosophers and statesmen.
    2. Writers and teachers.
    3. Business and government leaders.
    4. Economists and engineers.
    5. Farmers and journalists.

N. GENERALLY SPEAKING, I FIND A THEORY USEFUL IF IT:
    1. Seems related to other theories or ideas that I have learned.
    2. Explains things to me in a new way.
    3. Can systematically explain a number of related situations.
    4. Serves to clarify my own experience and observations.
    5. Has a practical and concrete application.

O. WHEN I READ AN ARTICLE ON A CONTROVERSIAL SUB-
    JECT, I PREFER THAT IT:
    1. Show the benefits to me for choosing a point of view.
    2. Set forth all the facts in the controversy.
    3. Logically outline the issues involved.
    4. Identify the values supported by the writer.
    5. Highlight both sides of the issue and clarify the conflict.

Please transfer your answers to the corresponding boxes on the last page of the
test.

P. IF I READ A BOOK OUTSIDE MY FIELD, I AM MOST LIKELY TO DO SO BECAUSE OF:

1. An interest in improving my professional knowledge. ☐
2. Having been told it would be useful by someone I respect. ☐
3. A desire to extend my general knowledge. ☐
4. A desire to get outside my field for a change. ☐
5. Curiosity to learn more about the specific subject. ☐

Q. WHEN I FIRST APPROACH A TECHNICAL PROBLEM, I AM MOST LIKELY TO:

1. Try to relate it to a broader problem or theory. ☐
2. Look for ways to get the problem solved quickly. ☐
3. Think of a number of opposing ways to solve it. ☐
4. Look for ways that others might have solved it. ☐
5. Try to find the best procedure for solving it. ☐

R. GENERALLY SPEAKING, I AM MOST INCLINED TO:

1. Find existing methods that work, and use them as well as possible. ☐
2. Speculate about how dissimilar methods might work together. ☐
3. Discover new and better methods. ☐
4. Find ways to make existing methods work in a new and better way. ☐
5. Figure out how existing methods ought to work. ☐

Please transfer your answers to the corresponding boxes on the next page.

1. Add boxes horizontally

2. Add box totals vertically

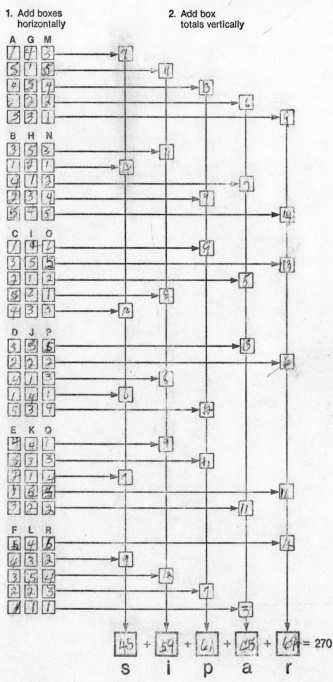

45 + 59 + 61 + 45 + 64 = 270

s   i   p   a   r

Orientation	I SYNTHESIST	II IDEALIST	III PRAGMATIST	IV ANALYST	V REALIST
Characterized by:	Integrative view Sees likeness in apparent unlikes Seeks conflict & synthesis Interested in change Speculative Data meaningless w/o interpretation	Assimilative or holistic view Broad range of views welcomed Seeks ideal solutions Interested in values Receptive Data & theory of equal value	Eclectic view "Whatever works" Seeks shortest route to payoff Interested in Innovation Adaptive Any data or theory that gets us there	Formal logic & deduction Seeks "one best way" Seeks models & formulas Interested in "scientific" solutions Prescriptive Theory and method over data	Empirical view & induction Relies on "facts" & expert opinion Seeks solutions that meet current needs Interested in concrete results Corrective Data over theory
Strengths:	Focus on underlying assumptions Points out abstract conceptual aspects Good at preventing over-agreement Best in controversial, conflict-laden situations Provides debate & creativity	Focus on process, relationships Points out values & aspirations Good at articulating goals Best in unstructured, value-laden situations Provides broad view, goals & standards	Focus on payoff Points out tactics & strategies Good at identifying impacts Best in complex, incremental situations Provides experiment & Innovation	Focus on method & plan Points out data & details Good at model-building & planning Best in structured, calculatable situations Provides stability & structure	Focus on facts & results Points out realities & resources Good at simplifying, "cutting through" Best in well-defined, objective situations Provides drive & momentum
Liabilities:	May screen out agreement May seek conflict unnecessarily May try too hard for change & newness May theorize excessively Can appear uncommitted	May screen out "hard" data May delay from too many choices May try too hard for "perfect" solutions May overlook details Can appear overly sentimental	May screen out long-range aspects May rush too quickly to payoff May try too hard for expediency May rely too much on what "sells" Can appear over-compromising	May screen out values & subjectives May over-plan, over-analyze May try too hard for predictability May be inflexible, overly cautious Can appear tunnel-visioned	May screen out disagreement May rush to over-simplified solutions May try too hard for consensus & immediate response May over-emphasize perceived "facts" Can appear too results-oriented

READING LIST

Anderson, J. R. *Language, Memory and Thought*. Erlbaum, 1976.

Bruner, Jerome S., Goodnow, J., and Austin, G. *A Study of Thinking*. New York: John Wiley and Sons, 1956.

Buchler, Justus. *The Concept of Method*. New York: Columbia University Press, 1961.

Church, J. *Language and the Discovery of Reality*. New York: Vintage Books, 1961.

Churchman, C. West. *Challenge to Reason*. New York: McGraw-Hill, 1968.

———*The Design of Inquiring Systems*. New York: Basic Books, 1971.

DeBono, E. *Lateral Thinking*. New York: Harper & Row, 1972.

Fromm, Erich. *Man for Himself*. New York: Fawcett Publications, 1947.

Holton, G. *Thematic Origins of Scientific Thought*. Harvard University Press, 1973.

Hough, R. *Captain Bligh and Mr. Christian*. New York: Dutton, 1973.

Inhelder, B., and Piaget, J. *The Growth of Logical Thinking from Childhood to Adolescence*. New York: Basic Books, 1958.

Kelly, G. A. *The Psychology of Personal Constructs*. New York: Norton, 1955.

Klein, George S. *Perception, Motives and Personality*. San Francisco: Jossey-Bass Publishers, 1970.

Lorsch, J., and Morse, J. *Organizations and Their Members: A Contingency Approach*. New York: Harper & Row, 1974.

Mahler, B. *Clinical Psychology and Personality—The Selected Papers of George Kelly*. New York: John Wiley and Sons, 1969.

Mason, Richard O. "A Dialectical Approach to Strategic Planning," *Management Science*, April 1969.

McKenney, J., and Keen, P. "How Managers' Minds Work," *Harvard Business Review*, Vol. 52, No. 3.

Mitroff, Ian I., and Pondy, Lois R. "On the Organization of Inquiry," *Public Administration Review*, September/October, 1974.

Neisser, U. *Cognition and Reality*. San Francisco: Freeman, 1976.

Rothenberg, A. "Creative Contradictions," *Psychology Today*, June 1979.

——*The Creative Process in Art, Science and Other Fields*. University of Chicago Press, 1979.

Schutz, W. Firo. *A Three Dimensional Theory of Interpersonal Behavior*. New York: Holt, Rinehart & Winston, 1958.

Snow, C. P. *Variety of Men*. New York: Charles Scribner's Sons, 1966.

Watson, J. *The Double Helix*. New York: Atheneum, 1968.

INDEX

"Abilene Paradox, The" (Harvey), 28
Abstract paintings, 76
Alinsky, Saul, 140–41
Altruism, 171
Ambiguity, 90
Ambivalence, 91
American Psychologist, The, 180n
Analysis, negative, 27–29, 60, 118, 153–54
Analyst-Idealists (AI), 166
Analyst-Pragmatists (AP), 87–88
Analyst-Realists (AR), 81–82
  Idealist-Pragmatists and, 87
  Pragmatist-Realists and, 85
  Synthesist-Idealists and, 82–83
Analysts (A), 8, 53–65, 79, 174, 180
  Analyst-Synthesists and, 89
  aspirations and, 157
  behavioral clues to thinking style of, 99
  characteristics of, 53–54
  chronological appearance in Western thought, 173, 174
  conceptualization strategy of, 179
  contingency approach and, 44
  Descartes as, 173
  developing skills of, 161–64
    attention to detail, 163–64
    constraint, 164
    data gathering, 162
    flowchart preparation, 162
    statistics or operations research, 161–62
    tolerating quantification, 163
  the Enlightenment and, 173
  environment and, 64
  functional rationality and, 175
  general situation most effective in, 147
  Idealists and, 14, 15, 38–39, 41, 58, 106

  incisiveness and, 166–67
  influencing, 105–11
    brainstorming, 128
    extensional questions, 109–10
    logical orderly proposals, 107–8
    need for data, 108–10
    providing feedback, 106–7
    surfacing the theory, 110–11
    thorough preparation, 107
  influencing techniques of, 96
  the i_nQ score and, 14–15
  as left-brain dominant people, 177
  Leibniz as, 173
  liabilities of, 62–65
  most common error of, 55
  negative analysis and, 27–28
  Pragmatists and, 13, 14, 15, 50, 56, 106, 116
  problems and, 15
  Realists and, 17, 56, 69, 76, 106, 113
  scientific method and, 173
  specifics and, 72
  stereotype of, 99
  strategies of, 54–62
    analysis of alternatives, 55–56
    charting the situation, 59–60
    conservative focusing, 58–59
    constructive nit-picking, 60–61
    deductive reasoning, 61–62
    search for best way, 54–55
    search for more data, 56–58
  strengths of, 62–65, 75, 142–45
    attention to detail, 143, 144–45
    step by step inquiry, 143–44
  symbolic logic and, 174
  Synthesists and, 15, 60, 106, 133
  theory and, 14–15
  thought processes of, 15, 53
  worldview and, 15
Analyst-Synthesists (AS), 88–89

Realists and, 13, 16–17
Singer as, 173
social experiment and, 173
stereotypes of, 99
strategies of, 44–50
  contingency planning, 44, 50
  experiment and innovation, 46
  looking for a short-range payoff,
    46–47, 159
  marketing approach, 49–50
  moving one step at a time,
    44–46
  tactical thinking, 47–49
strengths of, 50–52, 138–42
  opportunism, 139–40
  short-term payoffs, 141–42
  tactical leadership, 140–41
substantive vs. functional rationality and, 175–76
Synthesists and, 43, 46
Preemptive participation, 34–35
Problem solving
  Analysts and, 15
  Idealists and, 13, 34–35
Process philosophy, 173
Progoff, Ira, 68n
*Psychology of Personal Constructs,
The* (Kelly), 179

Quantification, 163
Questions
  dumb-smart, 22–23, 151
  extensional, 109–10

Radiologists, 144
Realists (R), 8, 10, 67–77, 79, 174,
  181
  abstract painting and, 76
  Analysts and, 17, 56, 69, 76, 106,
    113
  aspirations and, 157
  behavioral clues to thinking style
    of, 99
  Bentham as, 173
  characteristics of, 67–68
  chronological appearance in West-
    ern thought of, 173
  conceptualizing strategy of, 179
  concrete results and, 84–85
  developing skills of, 164–67
    concrete results, 164–65
    getting to the point, 166

    incisiveness, 166–67
    paraphrasing, 166
    resources, 165
  empiricism and, 16, 68, 173
  facts and, 16–17, 67
  functional rationality and, 175
  general situation most effective in,
    147
  humor of, 68
  Idealists and, 38–39, 41, 102, 114
    influencing, 104–5
    skill development, 156
  incisiveness of, 17, 67–68
  Industrial Revolution and, 173
  influencing, 111–16
    brainstorming, 128
    conciseness, 113
    encouraging appropriation,
      114–15
    getting to the point, 111–13,
      114
    giving control, 115–16
  influencing techniques of, 96
  the i_nQ score and, 16–17
  as left-brain dominant people, 177
  liabilities of, 75–77
  Locke as, 173
  motto of, 16, 77
  negative analysis and, 27
  Pragmatists and, 13, 16–17
  quantification and, 163
  stereotype of, 99
  strategies of, 68–75
    empirical discovery, 68
    getting to specifics, 71–72
    incisive correction, 74–75
    resource inventory, 70–71
    setting hard objectives, 69–70
    simplification, 72–73
    using expert opinion, 73–74
  strengths of, 75–77, 145–47
    as catalysts, 147
    energizing for organization, 145,
      147
    immediate practical solutions,
      145–46, 147
  Synthesists and, 16–17, 90–91,
    124
  thinking process of, 73–75
  utilitarianism and, 173
Reasoning, deductive, 61–62
Receptive listening, 35–36